Leicestershire Museums, Art Galleries and Records Service

THE NORMAN CONQUEST OF LEICESTERSHIRE AND RUTLAND: A REGIONAL INTRODUCTION TO DOMESDAY BOOK

(With a foreword by G. H. Martin, Keeper of the Public Records)

Edited by

CHARLES PHYTHIAN-ADAMS

*(Head of the Department of English Local History,
The University of Leicester)*

1986

1986 Leicestershire Museums Publication No. 73.
Leicestershire Museums, Art Galleries and Records Service

Typeset by Arrow Photoset, Leicester
Printed by de Voyle Litho, Leicester

Designed by Leicestershire Museums Design Section

ISBN 0 85022 200 1

FOREWORD

Domesday Book, nine hundred years old in 1986, is the first of the public records. William the Conqueror commissioned it at the end of 1085, and it seems to have been completed in its present form by the time of his death in 1087. Twenty years after his victory at Hastings William wished to know what were the resources of England and in whose hands they lay. His commissioners visited every part of the kingdom between the Channel in the south and the Tees and the Cumbrian fells in the north, armed with a questionnaire of which we still have the details. The information which they gathered was digested first in the form of regional surveys, and then in the neat double columns of the county surveys of which Leicestershire, and, under Nottinghamshire, *Roteland* are examples. Of the two parts of the work, long known as Great and Little Domesday, it seems that the text of Little Domesday, which covers Essex, Norfolk, and Suffolk and is dated 1086, represents the penultimate stage of the recension. The work was interrupted, almost certainly by William's death, before those counties could be assimilated in the form of the larger volume.

Domesday has been in official custody for the whole of its existence. In the Middle Ages it was regarded with awe as a definitive statement of titles to land, and especially of the extent of the king's estates. For the last three centuries it has been an object of study by historians and antiquaries. The celebration of its nongenary in 1986 is a tribute to its power and fascination as a book, as an instrument of administration, and as an historical text.

The entries for Rutland are scattered, a fact which reflects its peculiar status at the time of the survey. The seven folios devoted to Leicestershire (ff 230-236) present us with a unique picture of the county in the last years of the Old English kingdom and during the Conqueror's reign. They are organised in a familiar way, with the account of Leicester preceding the list of 44 holders of land and the opening entries for the king's lands. Like all the other parts of the work, however, they will repay closer study. Leicester was one of the Five Boroughs of the Danelaw, and an archetype of those Midland county towns which bear the name of the shire in which they stand. Like Lincoln, however, and unlike Derby, Nottingham, and Stamford which are returned as boroughs, it is described as a *civitas*, a city, probably as a tribute to its Roman origins, and perhaps to its history as a bishop's seat. The large estate of the bishop of Lincoln, which was later known as the Bishop's Fee, is another reminder of that connexion. The description of the town includes the seignorial properties attached to manors in the county, which may have secured marketing rights for their lords. It also refers to six churches, the only ones mentioned in Leicestershire, though as Breedon reminds us there were certainly others elsewhere in the county. The churches are another indication that Leicester was a place of consequence, a focus of trade as well as an administrative centre.

The influence of its earls was an important factor in the later history of Leicester. There was no earl in 1086, but Hugh of Grandmesnil, whose son became the first earl, was strongly established in the city and the shire. Domesday's account of his estates and the holdings of the king, of the great churches, and of other lords, reveals the patterns of settlement in eleventh-century Leicestershire, with a scattered occupation of the forest lands to the west of Leicester and much activity in the Wreake valley and the south-eastern lands. Domesday is usually the foundation of county topography, and the Leicestershire text has been closely studied by historians since Nichols made it widely available in his *History and Antiquities of Leicestershire* (1795). The celebration of the eight-hundredth anniversary of Domesday Book in 1886 marked an important stage in medieval studies, and in our whole understanding of that period in our past. The Leicestershire Record Office, in its present commemoration of a unique archival tradition, takes a further step on the road that the royal commissioners first travelled nine hundred years ago.

G. H. Martin,
Keeper of the Public Records

CONTENTS

List of insets

List of Contributors

Jill Bourne   (Extra-Mural Tutor in Local History)

Allen Chinnery   (Lately Deputy Director, Leicestershire Museums, Art Galleries and Records Service)

T. H. McK. Clough   (Keeper, Rutland County Museum)

Michael J. Moore   (Assistant Director, Leicestershire Museums, Art Galleries and Records Service)

David Parsons   (Senior Lecturer in the Department of Adult Education, The University of Leicester)

R. A. Rutland   (Keeper of Archaeology, Leicestershire Museum, Art Galleries and Records Service)

Daniel Williams   (Lecturer in the Department of History, The University of Leicester)

List of Figures

1. Domesday Book: The folio for the *Roteland* entry
2. Domesday Book: A typical entry in the Leicestershire folios
3. The castle at Hallaton
4. The major cultural divisions of England in the early eleventh century
5. Territorial divisions of the region: Sokes, wapentakes and hundreds
6. Connections between Leicester and its countryside
7. A possible Anglo-Saxon estate: The Langtons
8. A possible Anglo-Saxon estate: Toki's estate (Hallaton)
9. A possible Anglo-Saxon estate: Claybrooke
10. A possible Anglo-Saxon estate: Market Bosworth
11. A possible Anglo-Saxon estate: Lyddington
12. Family tree of the House of Leofric
13. The Earldoms in 1065
14. Origins of the Conquerors
15. The distribution of castle sites c. 1150
16. The agricultural sub-regions of Leicestershire and Rutland
17. Clergy and churches in 1086
18. St Nicholas, Leicester
19. St Bartholomew, Foston
20. Distribution of pre-Conquest carved stonework in Leicestershire and Rutland
21. Domesday Leicester
22. Silver Pennies of Eadward the Confessor and William the Conqueror

Acknowledgments

The Editor would particularly like to thank Harold Fox, Mary Ball and Tim Clough for information provided; Tom Cain for suggestive comments; Iris Browning for many kindnesses that have made the preparation of this book if not quite, at least almost tolerable; Anne Barker for drafting maps; Edward Moody and Alan Birdsall for their outstanding helpfulness and expertise in preparing and designing the manuscript for publication; Muriel Phillips and Audrey Riley for so kindly typing parts of it; and especially Dorothy Brydges, not only for her imperturbability in the face of both the editor's handwriting and savage deadlines, but also for her exceptional accuracy and speed when typing the greater part of the manuscript in these circumstances.

Introduction

Editor

Even on its nine-hundredth anniversary, the formidable achievement of Domesday Book is more a matter for respectful recognition than for celebration. Leaving aside all the other significances it may have come subsequently to possess, the Great Survey in essence remains a monument to the subjection of the English people, and to the iron will of the man who was the last to conquer them nearly a millennium ago. It is thus more appropriate to *mark* such an anniversary, as is being done by the Leicestershire Record Office in conjunction with the Public Record Office, in what can only be, however, a temporary exhibition which illustrates and blends the major national and regional themes of that period. To help elaborate on the contents of the exhibition and to provide a more lasting comment on the contents of Domesday Book, this publication has been designed to appear simultaneously.

The fascination of Domesday lies in the manner in which it confronts us. Like a still photograph, before our very eyes it freezes into somewhat blurred immobility an entire state and whole society that existed in this land almost a thousand year ago. Like any such picture, it challenges the curious to wonder what went before the portrait was taken, and what followed after. In this short book we shall try to explore what is now known about these matters in a series of interpretative chapters which focus on the central problems of the Domesday record in the national and, above all, in the regional context. By the end, the reader should have gained an up-to-date view not only on the effects of the Norman Conquest and the nature of life in late-eleventh century Leicestershire and Rutland, but also on some of the technical matters which face every student of Domesday. As such, this publication hopefully provides a starting-point for all those coming to this great record for the first time.

To attempt this, however, we must take a perspective far longer than the 20 years which separate 1086 from 1066. In Domesday are to be discerned not one, but two alien impositions on the native society of the East Midlands – the first, Viking; the second Norman-French – over a period of 200 years. As we shall see, the effects of the latter conquest are incomprehensible without some understanding of what the former also meant. Similarly, it should be stressed that so far as the implications of the Norman occupation are concerned, the only significance of the year 1086, lies in the fact that it was then that the unprecedented census since called Domesday Book was taken; of itself, the date 1086 has no wider meaning at all. It is for that reason that in the pages which follow we shall also have to look forward occasionally from 1086 even into the middle years of the twelfth century.

In this book, therefore, the subject is broken down into three broad parts according to three appropriately contrasted chronological perspectives. In Part I are discussed both the short-term impact of the Norman Conquest and the subsequent making of the Domesday Survey itself. With a time-scale thus largely restricted to the reign of William I (1066–1087), it so provides the essential starting-point from which the further implications of the Domesday record may be pursued. Part II, takes a far wider period for reference. It looks both backwards and forwards from 1086: back even before the Scandinavian settlement in order to understand the subsequent nature of Anglo-Danish society in the region and its evolving institutions, which the Normans in part disrupted through conquest, and in part inspected through the Domesday survey; forward, so far as some of these themes are concerned, into the century after Domesday. In broad terms, Part II thus ranges chronologically from the ninth to the twelfth centuries. From these essential discussions it is hoped, finally, that the reader may acquire a general framework of understanding with which to return in Part III both to the late-eleventh century in particular and to the unrivalled picture of the region – both town and country alike – which Domesday provides for us at that time.

The text of Domesday Book has exercised some of the finest historical minds of the last century, but while much has been made clearer as a result of this scholarly activity, it cannot be claimed that firm solutions have been reached on every point. For reasons of space – and to spare the reader – it will be appreciated that many of these complex matters have had to be suppressed here, while in a field where problems are infinitely disputable (as is inevitable in any major code-breaking exercise), the contributors to this work have had room only to record, rather than argue in detail, views that others might regard as controversial. Careful readers should soon spot such differing points of emphasis, and it is to be hoped that the highly selective bibliography included below will help to indicate to them how these problems may be pursued further. In the case of a handful of matters, however, it has been felt that some elaboration should be provided. The text is therefore punctuated with occasional "insets" which provide supplementary information on a few key subjects of which the curious reader will wish to be aware. In these, and elsewhere in this book, the contributors have not hesitated to look more widely than the region itself. While the focus of the work is on Leicestershire and Rutland (the balance between them being broadly determined by their relative sizes), it cannot be stressed too strongly that the wider contexts simply have to be understood before the experiences of the region itself even begin to be comprehensible.

This publication was projected originally by the Leicestershire Record Office, and progress had been made both in the selection of some of the themes contained herein, and in the choice of contributors, when the present editor took over responsibility, by invitation, on 26 September 1985. Thanks to the diligence and cooperation of all the contributors, this considerably expanded and redesigned version of what previously had been intended, has been brought to a written conclusion within fifteen weeks. There has thus been no time for that overall re-assessment of the Domesday evidence for the region which is so badly needed. By introducing Domesday hopefully to a wider audience, however, perhaps others may now be encouraged to undertake that task.

Important Note to the Reader

T.R.E. = (*Tempore Regis Edwardi*) At the time of King Edward (Eadweard)
T.R.W. = At the time of King William

Domesday contains numerous other technical terms which can only be explained in the following text in their most appropriate contexts. To aid the reader, therefore, an index to the passages where these terms are defined will be found at the end of this publication. In addition, bracketed page numbers in the text itself – e.g. (p.9–10) – should also help the reader to cross-reference from one subject to another. The spelling of personal names in any study of this period, moreover, invariably poses problems to both reader and writer. Since the subject of this work has to do with a clash between cultures, it has been thought best to give expression to it by systematically using the authentic, and stronger sounding spellings of pre-Conquest names that are to be found in a well-known dictionary (Olof von Feilitzen, *The Pre-Conquest Personal Names of Domesday Book*, Nomina Germanica, Uppsala, 1937), so that the somewhat pallid modernised versions of names such as Edmund, Ethelred and Canute, here become Eadmund, Aethelred and Knut. For the same reason, the alien names of the continental leaders of the occupying force are deliberately given with reference to the easily identifiable modern spellings of the places whence they came. In the absence of footnotes, the reader should realise that where translations from supporting documents are not those of individual contributors, the best and most reliable modern translations have been used, *viz.*: *The Anglo-Saxon Chronicle*, transl. with an introduction by G. N. Garmonsway, London, 1953; *English Historical Documents, I, c. 500–1042*, ed. Dorothy Whitelock, London, 1968; *English Historical Documents, II, 1042–1189*, ed. D. C. Douglas and G. W. Greenaway, 2nd edn., 1981; and *The Ecclesiastical History of Orderic Vitalis*, ed. and transl. Marjorie Chibnall, Oxford, 1969–80.

THE NORMAN CONQUEST
OF LEICESTERSHIRE AND RUTLAND:
A REGIONAL INTRODUCTION
TO DOMESDAY BOOK

inset 1 The Technology of Battle:

(Cover Illustration: The Battle of Hastings) . . . . Michael J. Moore

The Bayeaux Tapestry provides a remarkable contemporary record of eleventh century warfare, the accuracy of which has been confirmed by archaeology. Commissioned by Bishop Odo of Bayeux, it was almost certainly designed by an Englishman familiar with the panoply of war.

The artist has recorded the equipment of the armies in some detail although his stylised draughtsmanship on occasion requires interpretation. The warriors of both armies wear the ubiquitous hooded mail shirt, the hem reaching to the knee or below, its arms to the elbow or just above. They wear conical helmets which sit high on the head. Each helmet is equipped with a "nasal", a metal strip projecting from the lower rim to protect the warrior's nose and face.

Nearly every warrior on the tapestry carries a shield but here for the first time the equipment of Saxon and Norman sometimes differs. The Normans carry long kite-shaped shields while a number of Saxons bear circular shields (not shown in illustration). The wooden shields were strengthened by a covering of leather glued to the front and rear face and by metal binding to protect their edge. Many, if not all the shields shown are decorated on their front face. These designs and motifs were not true heraldry intended to identify the bearer, but simple decoration.

In weaponry a further distinction between Saxon and Norman can be seen on parts of the tapestry. While the Normans fight with sword, spear and occasionally mace; in the Saxon ranks the axe tends to feature prominently. In Anglo-Saxon England an earlier tradition of foot-combat had survived: the English nobility might ride to the field, but there they would dismount to fight shoulder to shoulder behind their shield wall (see cover). For them, therefore, the long-helved war axe was an ideal weapon. Thrown, wielded with one hand or two, it could cut with ease through shields and armour that would turn a sword blade. The Normans by contrast had adopted mounted combat with its combination of mobility and shock. Few foot-soldiers could resist for long the impact of horse and heavily armoured man, or continue to fight effectively while protecting themselves against the blows rained down by a man in the saddle. Norman armour had to some degree evolved to match this method of combat. A number of knights on the tapestry wear mail hose to protect their legs, which were vulnerable to attack from foot-soldiers, while the kite-shaped shield protected them from throat to knee.

PART I DOMESDAY BOOK AND THE NORMAN CONQUEST 1066–1086

Daniel Williams

The middle years of the eleventh century witnessed one of the most profound upheavals in the whole of English history: what amounted to a transition from the Teutonic and Scandinavian cultures that had dominated Britain for centuries past to the Frankish and Latin culture that was to dominate the kingdom of England for centuries to come.

The crucible of this traumatic though momentous transition is to be found in the three great battles of the year 1066. Fittingly, the most remembered of these three encounters was the last and most positive, the Battle of Hastings, which secured the kingdom of the English for Duke William of Normandy and brought with it England's destiny as an integral part of Latin Christendom. The earlier northern battles of Fulford and Stamford Bridge are the least remembered, yet they both severed the kingdom's links with Scandinavia (which went back over two centuries), and, in an equally negative way, by fearful attrition helped to secure the finality of the Norman victory in the south. Indeed the cumulative carnage of these three battles and their aftermath resulted in the virtual genocide of the Anglo-Saxon military aristocracy, the royal house of Godwine supported by its earls, thegns and house-carls: an heroic end, worthy of any Saga. Through defeat at Fulford and through victory at Stamford Bridge, this decimated and mortally wounded warrior class took its Viking oppressors with it and so ended two hundred years of piracy and invasion from the North. *The Anglo-Saxon Chronicle* with consummate pride records the stark logistics of these two battles 'fought within five nights'. Before the first two of these battles, Harald Hardraada, King of Norway, and the renegade Earl Tosti, with over 300 longships sailed up the Humber. After Stamford Bridge, the shattered and humbled survivors of this last Viking invasion made their peace with the victorious King Harald of England and departed in only 24 ships.

Tragically, within a few weeks, the last Anglo-Saxon king and most of his thegns lay dead upon a hillside near Hastings, thus completing the cycle of attrition which destroyed the flower of the Anglo-Saxon thegns with their military *heriots* (death-duties) of horses, weapons and armour: men like the five thegns who had held the rich manor of Loughborough; the three thegns who held a part of Swinford; or perhaps the grander Aethelric son of Maergeat who had held extensive estates within the two Leicestershire wapentakes of Guthlaxton and Gartree. In the forfeiture that followed the Conquest, the latter's lands were transferred *en bloc* to the Norman, Robert of Vessey. Those who survived the battles were faced with the alternatives of exile or submission with its consequential loss of status. Little wonder so many were to rise against their Norman lords between 1066 and 1070. The failure of William's qualified appeasement, followed by the ruthless and murderous suppression of Anglo-Saxon resistance during those four years, completed the virtual extinction of this warrior class. By the Domesday Survey of 1086, less than 8% of the land of England was still held by surviving thegns, and most of those are recorded at the lowest levels of the new feudal, tenurial hierarchy.

It was more probably this situation rather than the English lack of castles (as was suggested by the chronicler, Orderic Vitalis) which enabled the Normans finally to hold down their newly conquered kingdom.

The warriors of Harald Godwinson destroyed the last serious Scandinavian threat and with their axes severed links with that world, but at such a cost as to enable William of Normandy to destroy the remnants of their military power and make good his claims to a new kingdom.

Even so, the Conqueror's task of securing that kingdom was to take him virtually the rest of his days at the cost of further great loss of life, both Norman and Anglo-Saxon. The process of securing the kingdom was to be a piecemeal military solution of territorial integration through the establishment of palatinate earldoms and feudal Honours centred upon castles, like the ones established at Warwick, Leicester and Nottingham during William's punitive campaign of 1068–9. In this way the Conqueror forged a political nation out of the disparate elements of Wessex, Mercia and Northumbria, a nation fringed by the opportunistic hostility of the Welsh and the Scots, and intersected by Danish settlement.

The success of this policy, not finally completed until the reign of Henry I, made William the greatest *Bretwealda* ("Britain-ruler") of them all. Even the writer of the Anglo-Saxon Chronicle was to acknowledge:

This King William . . . was a very wise man and very powerful and more worshipful and stronger than any predecessors of his had been.

Having secured the boundaries of his new kingdom of the English, the Conqueror strengthened beyond all previous measures the internal bastions of the state; the crown, the church and the aristocracy. All three were integrated into a feudal society based upon Frankish practice, adapted to ensure the success of national monarchy. Here again the demise of virtually the entire Anglo-Saxon ruling class gave William the opportunity to enfief his own Norman and French followers and set up the rudiments of their continental feudalism: the mounted knight, military tenure, vassalic commendation (formal allegiance to some lord in return for his protection) and the castle, all under the control of a wealthy and powerful royal dynasty.

That was the extent of the transformation. That was all that was needed. In every other respect, what remained of the society, culture, administration and economy of his conquered kingdom was far superior to anything William had encountered in Normandy. Norman England was the Anglo-Saxon state under a new, ruthless and vigorous regime. The Anglo-Danish political structure of the great earldoms was adapted to the Franco-Norman structure of more numerous feudal units: the large Honours that came eventually to constitute twelfth century earldoms like that of Leicester; and lesser honours that eventually coalesced into the twelfth century feudal baronies held of the king by knight service, which included the ecclesiastical estates of primates, bishops, abbots and priors. These feudal Honours established a territorial stability and a cohesion that was to endure throughout the medieval period, acquiring over the centuries, an atavistic hierarchy of personal loyalty between the lord, the vassals and the tenants of the Fee. Equally, a fundamental set of rules and *modus vivendi* was established between the Crown and the feudal Honour which was to be a factor of political stability ignored by kings at their peril.

Such a transition at a time of acute political instability, involving a French feudal aristocracy steeped in practices of internecine feuding and private warfare, inevitably led to protracted disputes and territorial or jurisdictional claims that spilled over into the kind of violence and intimidation so graphically described by the Abingdon chronicler. This problem was compounded by the fractionalisation of landholding in early Norman England, and resulted in numerous disputes which were still in the process of litigation by the mid-1080's. Indeed the collection of the 1084 geld – an Anglo-Saxon land-tax – also revealed the chaotic state of land tenure and therefore of land values during this period of transition.

All these diverse factors were brought to a head by the cost and the billeting of a large French mercenary force recruited by the King to meet the threat – that was not to materialise – of a further Scandinavian invasion in 1085. These immediate circumstances were the catalyst that set into motion a detailed and comprehensive survey of the crown's fiscal assets and a definitive examination of landholding in England. The result of this survey, known to us as Domesday Book, presents the extremely complex historical problem of turning a tax-assessment into a unique picture of eleventh-century life. The problem is exacerbated by the very uniqueness of Domesday Book as an historical source. Paradoxically, the period from 1070 until the Conqueror's death in 1087, the period reflected in the Domesday Book, is one of the most sparsely documented in the whole medieval period. We have to fall back once again, as in the dark eras of the tenth century upon a somewhat depleted narrative of the Anglo-Saxon Chronicle supplemented by twelfth century works like Orderic Vitalis's *Ecclesiastical History* and Florence of Worcester's *Chronicle*.

Under the year 1085 the Peterborough version of the Anglo-Saxon Chronicle records the apprehension caused by the anticipated Danish invasion of the North and the King's draconian preparations to meet it; the devastations of the coastal areas of the north-east and the billeting of his mercenary army. The court celebrated Christmas at Gloucester and shortly after the King:

> had important deliberations and exhaustive discussions with his council about this land (i.e. England) and how it was peopled, and with what sort of men. Then he sent his men all over England into every shire to ascertain how many hundreds of 'hides' of land there were in each shire, and how much land and live-stock the king himself owned, in the country, and what annual dues were lawfully his from each shire. He also had it recorded . . . what or how much each man who was a landholder here in England had in land or in live-stock, and how much money it was worth. So very thoroughly did he have the inquiry carried out that there was not a single 'hide', not one virgate of land, not even . . . one ox, nor one cow, nor one pig which escaped notice in his survey. And all the surveys were subsequently brought to him.

In addition to giving the background of events, the Anglo-Saxon Chronicle emphasises the thoroughness of the Domesday Survey although this is not always reflected, as in the case of Leicestershire, in the actual text of the Domesday Book itself.

The Worcester *Chronicle*'s observations are briefer but with certain interesting and useful additional elements. The annal for 1086 records:

> King William caused all England to be surveyed; namely the quantity of land possessed by each of his barons, the number of knights' fees, the number of hides of land, the number of villeins, the number of beasts, yea, the amount of ready money which each possessed in all his kingdom from the greatest to the least, and how much rent each property was able to return: and the land was sorely vexed with the murders which proceeded therefrom.

Though there are some difficulties about this interpretation it does emphasise the feudal character of land tenure in post-Conquest England. In addition, the comment about the violence that followed from the consequences of such a survey can be corroborated and enlarged upon by Robert Bishop of Hereford's comments, 'And the land was vexed with much violence arising from the collection of royal taxes'. Both these near-contemporary sources cast doubt upon the much later, benign comments of the author of *A Dialogue Concerning the Exchequer* (1177–9):

> In simple language they set down their findings in a book, so that everyone might be content with his own rights and not seek with impunity to encroach upon the rights of others.

That was neither the purpose nor the consequences of the Domesday Survey, though it does reflect one of its more influential historical myths.

The best sources for the actual details of the administrative processes involved in the 1086 survey are the brief though apposite comments of Henry of Huntingdon's *History of the English* for the early twelfth century:

> This most powerful king sent his justices through every shire . . . and caused an inquiry to be made by sworn inquest how many hides (that is to say, ploughlands each sufficient for one plough in the year) there were in each village, and what livestock. He also made enquiry what each city, castle, township, village, marsh and wood was wont to render each year. All these writings in records (cartis scripta) were brought to the king, and they are preserved in the treasury to this day.

And finally the most detailed surviving description of the actual form the Domesday Inquiry took, is that of *The Inquest of Ely*, written shortly (?) after 1086:

> Here follows the inquiry concerning lands
> which the king's barons made according to
> the oath of the sheriff of the shire and of
> all the barons and their Frenchmen, and of
> and whole hundred court – the priest,
> reeve and 6 villeins from each village.
> They inquired what the manor was
> called, who held it in the time of King
> Eadward [tempore regis Edwardi or T.R.E.:
> that is before 1066], who holds it
> now [1086]
> how many hides there are
> how many ploughs in demesne
> [the land of the lord of the manor]
> and how many belonging to the men [of the
> village]
> how many villeins
> how many cottars
> how many slaves
> how many freemen
> how many sokemen
> how much woodland
> how much meadow
> how much pasture
> how many mills
> how many fisheries
> how much has been added to, or taken away
> from, [the manor]
> what it used to be worth altogether
> what it is worth now
> [and] how much each free man and soke-
> man had and has
> All this to be recorded thrice: that is as
> it was in the time of King Eadward, as it
> was when King William gave [the manor], and
> as it is now.
> And it was also noted whether more could
> be taken from the [manor] than is now being
> taken.

From these detailed comments, the purpose of the 1086 survey becomes clear. It was to provide a reasonable precise record of the assets and taxable wealth of the king's subjects which could be compared with extant Anglo-Saxon records relating to assessments of liability for danegeld. Such an undertaking was obviously necessary after such a great upheaval in land-ownership as that brought about by the Conquest. The King clearly wished to exact at least as much tax from his French and Norman landowners as his predecessors had exacted from their Anglo-Danish subjects. Earlier sources like the *Northamptonshire Geld Roll* of *c.* 1072–8 throw light upon the fiscal procedure for taxation during the reign of Eadward the Confessor. It was relatively unsophisticated but functional. Each shire was assessed upon a rounded-up number of geldable units of land which were then divided between the Hundreds or Wapentakes (p.8) and the villages or estates. This somewhat arbitrary procedure was based upon a unit of land known as a hide, or in the counties of the Danelaw as the carucate, an area of about 120 acres (p.7). In hidated regions, the precise amount of land assessed for tax purposes was rounded up into units of five or ten, along decimal lines. In areas of the Danelaw like Leicestershire or northern Rutland, the unit of individual land assessment was rounded up into combinations of six or twelve carucates, according to a duodecimal system. That this was the case in Leicestershire can be confirmed by comparisons with the *c.* 1130 *Leicestershire Survey* (p.8).

This method must have worked effectively enough for the Norman kings of the post-Conquest period and their administrations not to tinker with it. William applied it in an equally arbitrary way to his subjects, French and English, except perhaps, as can be implied from the *Ely Inquest*, he wished to increase the geld's yield at the expense of his subjects. It is also quite possible that valuations were rounded up or down by the compilers of Domesday Book according to the will or favour of the King. Consequently the first normal Domesday Book entry for each manor or vill is an estimated land measure of geld liability worked out from earlier Anglo-Saxon assessments for that particular estate.

Professor V. H. Galbraith's researches have revealed the stages of the actual survey that resulted in Domesday Book. Roving commissions of royal clerks, ecclesiastics and magnates set out on at least seven different shire circuits to cover the whole of England south of the Tees. (The Leicestershire circuit included also Oxfordshire, Warwickshire, Northamptonshire and possibly Staffordshire. *Roteland*, by contrast, lay in the same circuit as the shires of Huntingdon, Derby, Nottingham, York and Lincoln.) They carried with them to each shire court a 'return' already endorsed with a list of major landowners within the county and the former total of geldable land from earlier records. The community was asked the questions set out in the *Ely Inquisition*, or a variation of them, and their answers were written down on the 'return' under the names of the holders of land in a fixed sequence beginning with an entry for the shire town, the list of principal landowners, then the details of their holdings from the king right down to vassals or tenants. These original 'returns' when brought back to the royal clerks at Winchester, comprised a vast agglomeration of parchment documents from which the two books of the Domesday Survey were compiled, but which, unfortunately for later historians, was afterwards destroyed.

Thus all the scribe at Winchester had to do, under the supervision of the royal clerks following the instructions of the royal council, was to copy out these 'returns' on the folios of Domesday Book in their preordained sequence. In Galbraith's words, the scribe's 'main task lay in the process of abbreviation'. At this point many of the problems later associated with the study of the

Domesday Survey may have begun when that task – vital to the final form of the record – was carried out within a comparatively short space of time under pressure. It is this fact that accounts for most of the inaccuracies and omissions, many of which, studies of related documents like *The Book of Exeter* suggest, were not present upon the now destroyed returns. A detailed examination of the actual manuscript of Domesday Book reveals the elements of haste and textual compression that occurred when the entries for the Leicestershire circuit had to be squeezed into a 60 line page of writing whereas the norm for earlier entries was a more expansive 44. This naturally resulted in considerably more omissions and indeed inaccuracies than are to be found in the more fully recorded entries like those for Middlesex, Huntingdon and Buckingham. In the case of Leicestershire, or the northern part of the county, many of these omissions can be corrected by the supplementation of the *Leicestershire Survey*.

From all this it will be gathered that the purpose of Domesday Book was essentially fiscal and administrative: to assess the wealth and liabilities, taxation and military, of the Conqueror's subjects within the novel feudal and social hierarchy of Norman England. Consequently, other important features of the survey carried out twenty years after the Conquest become apparent. The record reflects the dominance and preponderance of the Franco-Norman conquerors – a new ruling class almost exclusively alien, and of great landed wealth. In particular, the Norman aristocracy as a group were much wealthier than their Anglo-Saxon predecessors and very much wealthier than they had been as Norman or French lords and knights before 1066. As recent research has shown, the tenants-in-chief, the principal landowners recorded in each Domesday shire-entry, not only belonged to a small and influential aristocratic clique, but were for the most part members of a tightly knit kinship-group centred upon the Norman ruling dynasty, its favourites and retainers.

Below this feudal, alien ruling class, the Domesday Survey reveals essentially intact, the Anglo-Danish peasant society that had inhabited England for generations, even centuries, a society bound up in the economic conditions of agrarian life that had also prevailed for generations before the Conquest. This was in fact a generally thriving and resilient arable-based agrarian economy in which the indicator of wealth and taxable income was the number of heavy ploughs pulled by their teams of six to eight oxen. The specific questions answered in the survey illustrate the sophisticated husbandry practised upon an Anglo-Danish estate. The vill itself was a functional unit of agricultural labour, with its mill, its plough-lands in the form of ridge and furrow in the open fields, its precious meadow and pasture, its woodlands and waste. Nor should it be forgotten that there was a fundamental distinction between surplus and subsistence farming implied in the division between demesne land and that of the peasantry who worked it in addition to their own (p.17).

Above the indigenous peasantry, came the foreigners grafted onto these Anglo-Danish roots by conquest: the Frenchmen and the knights or, in Latin, *milites*. The two terms may be synonymous; or "Frenchman" may indicate some type of colonist, and the latter term, the rough and troublesome lower ranks of the still evolving knightly class of Norman England – the brutal soldiery who caused the unsavoury riot at the Conqueror's coronation, and who should be regarded as quite distinct from the more upper-class vavassours, knights and vassals actually named as subtenants of land in Domesday Book. Many of these had considerable landed estates and possessed Honours of their own right elsewhere. For all that, in 1086, these uncouth warriors fought on horseback like their betters and were technically and actually *milites*, that is knights, not men-at-arms as they are sometimes described in translations of Domesday Book (p.24). The Latin word *armiger* (an esquire) was not used until the third decade of the twelfth century, by which time social and military distinctions had become more precise.

1. Domesday Book: The folio for the *Roteland* entry, showing the two-column lay-out of the survey. There is an introductory paragraph on the taxation of the area in general, followed by lists of manors marked "M" under the names of each of the two wapentakes: Alfnodestov (Alstoe) and Martineslei (Martinsley). The numbers in the left-hand margin refer to the tenants-in-chief concerned: thus if I refers to the King, II relates to the Countess Judith and so on. What look like crossings-out on a black and white photograph are actually drawn in red ink in the original as are the elaborations of the initial letter of "In" at the beginning of each paragraph. In this way each entry might be quickly distinguished.

2. Domesday Book: A typical entry in the Leicestershire folios (f.231a) under the name of the fifth tenant-in-chief to be listed, Peterborough Abbey. Translated and extended it reads line by line as follows:

V   **THE LAND OF ST PETER OF BURGH**

THE ABBEY OF BURGH holds in (West) Langton 5 carucates of land
less 2 bovates. There is land for 5 ploughs. In demesne there is 1 (plough); and
       9 villeins
with 2 bordars have 3 ploughs. 8 acres of meadow and 5 acres of woodland
       (are) there.
It (the estate) was worth 10 shillings. Now (it is valued at) 40 shillings.
       Ailmarus (Aethelmaer) held it freely in the Time of King Eadweard.

Within this essential background of historical context and survey structure, some specific details of the Leicestershire portions of Domesday Book may be briefly examined. It has already been noted that the Leicestershire 'returns' were fairly drastically abbreviated and compressed in their final form upon the Domesday manuscript. This, coupled with many obvious errors and omissions, presents a number of seemingly intractable problems for the local historian. According to *The Ely Inquest* the final entry for most manors in the Domesday Survey should give three valuations: before 1066 (*T.R.E.*); later; now. In many counties, for example Warwickshire, those three valuations are given. In the Leicestershire entry there are only two. The abbreviation *T.R.E.* is also conspicuous by its usual absence. But are we to conclude, as did earlier Domesday scholars like Maitland and Stenton, that the "then" entry refers not to pre-1066 but to the period (perhaps 1068–70) when the Conqueror actually granted out each manor? This may be so but to construct, as Stenton does, a further hypothesis upon this first hypothesis, that the *vasta* or "waste" recorded for parts of Leicestershire, in conjunction with what Maitland has described as the low 'prairie values' of some adjacent manors, reflects the devastation caused by the Conqueror's army marching from Warwick to Nottingham in 1068, seems to stretch historical credulity. 'Prairie values' may in fact reflect only some form of administrative fiscal juggling at Winchester or, equally possible, the under-exploitation of manors in the least populated parts of the county (p.32). Again waste, *vasta* or *vastata*, is capable of a number of meanings other than devastation, and in particular of the more mundane, medieval meaning of uncultivated or unproductive land (p.26). At any event, such precarious hypotheses as the tracing of the Conqueror's 'storm path' of devastation in 1068 from a series of Domesday entries, leave the reader with a sense of ingenuity rather than conviction.

For all its pitfalls and imperfections, in the context of eleventh-century records Domesday Book remains absolutely unique in its breadth and detail. There is simply nothing comparable to it in English, European or even world history for that period. It was the unique product of a unique cultural mix: the advanced and sophisticated agrarian economy and administrative techniques of Anglo-Saxon and Dane galvanized by the extraordinary vigour and drive of Norman domination within the singular context of the Conquest; and a King who demanded to know certain things, and who was in control of an administration which was capable, if pushed (and pushed it was), of supplying him with answers on a hitherto unprecedented scale.

To judge this achievement restrospectively does less than justice to it. The question historians ought to ask of Domesday Book is not how accurate it was, but how accurate could it have been in the context of other eleventh-century records. The answer to that question highlights the achievement of the Survey and casts carping criticisms of detail into the background. The scale of this achievement was to be recognised by later medieval generations in the very title they attached to it. Within a century, the practical and comprehensive guide for royal administrators and lawyers in matters of tax assessment and land tenure, then known as the *Book of Winchester*, was to become known by its more awesome title of Domesday Book. Why this happened is explained to us by someone who really should have known – Richard Fitz Nigel, a direct descendant of the Conqueror, Bishop of London and Treasurer of England – in words that quaintly reflect the colonial aspect of Norman England. In his *Dialogue Concerning the Exchequer* this scholarly product of the further advances of twelfth century royal administration writes that:

The natives (indigenis) *called this book by the metaphor 'Domesday', that is the Day of Judgement. For just as that strict, dread and final examination cannot be overturned by any skilful cavil, so also, when there occurs in the realm a dispute concerning facts recorded therein, when an appeal is made to that book the evidence cannot be set aside or evaded with impunity.*

Already, within three generations, the myth of Domesday Book had been born. History had changed its function from fiscal to judicial. But that was to come. In the last year of the Conqueror's reign, the Domesday Survey was being used by the king and his sheriffs as a record for extortion.

Crown copyright. Ministry of Defence.

3. The castle at Hallaton (probably built for the Domesday tenant-in-chief, Geoffrey Alselin). All such castles were similar in design: a high steep-sided mound or motte, its summit surmounted by a watch-tower and encircled by a palisade, overlooked an enclosure, the bailey, fortified with ditch, bank and palisade which protected the domestic buildings – a timber-framed hall, stables, barn, smithy and sometimes perhaps a chapel and a separate kitchen. Motte and watch-tower formed a last redoubt to which the castle defenders could retreat if the bailey was over-run. (See also fig. 15.)   MJM.

PART II   REGIONAL BACKGROUNDS TO DOMESDAY BOOK

1. LEICESTERSHIRE AND RUTLAND: CONTEXTS, ORIGINS AND THE DOMESDAY RECORD

Introduction . . . . Editor

In broad terms, the territories of Leicestershire and Rutland may have comprised identifiable administrative units long before they became known as counties. Even in that fitfully documented period between the departure of the Romans and the onslaught of the Vikings, it is possible that in both areas, some continuing sense of territorial unity may have survived from yet earlier times: in the case of Leicester's territory, as a province of the Middle Angles which later became a diocese within the ambit of an expanding kingdom of Mercia; in the case of Rutland's, because at some point it may conceivably have become the traditional dower land of the Mercian Queens.

In 865, however, a great Danish army landed in East Anglia. Eight years later, Viking long boats penetrated through to the upper navigable reaches of the old course of the river Trent and their crews entrenched themselves for the winter at Repton, the cult-centre and mausoleum of the Mercian royal house. The king of Mercia was replaced by a puppet ruler and in 877, the victors appear to have parcelled out the East Midlands generally for settlement. Despite the subsequent military successes in the first half of the tenth century of their English opponents, and especially the rulers of Wessex, it was therefore from 877, or shortly after, that the peoples of much of central-eastern England came to be marked out as a distinctively separate part of the English nation.

It is impossible to understand the Domesday record of this region indeed without recognising the fact that for the preceding 200 years or so, the area as a whole was regarded by outsiders as "Danish". New Scandinavian lords took over English estates or created new ones. They brought with them a different system of social rank (the highest below that of king being the rank of *jarl* which later emerged in the Old English vocabulary as *eorl* or earl). The Danish tongue so permeated English speech that not only the names of many places, but also local dialects and accents were permanently altered. The Danes appear to have developed their own agricultural and fiscal terms: the "ploughland" (latinised by the Domesday scribes into *carucata*, hence carucate) – an area notionally taken to represent 100 or 120 acres which was subdivisible into eight "oxgangs" (latinised into *bovata*, hence bovate), each of which theoretically represented the holding of a man who could supply one ox to the average plough-team of 8 oxen. The Danes had their own unit of monetary account, the *ora* (inset 4). Even the coins they were licensed to mint by English kings in the tenth century did not, until 973, bear the imprint of the king's head as did silver pennies elsewhere in England. Above all, the Danes boasted their own system of law ("Dane law" as opposed to West Saxon or Mercian law, see fig. 4). As late as 962–3, and despite his overlordship of Danish England, King Eadgar is to be found legislating for his Scandinavian subjects in these terms: "it is my will that there should be in force among the Danes such good laws as they best decide on."

The Five Boroughs and the English crown

To judge from other Danish areas, such as those around Bedford, Huntingdon and Northampton, the manner in which Scandinavian settlement was enforced in a region was simple. A district (broadly equivalent to a later county area) would be dominated from a fortified centre (in all these cases, the later county town) around, and near to which, would settle a Danish army or *here* with its own periodic assembly, and under the control of a *jarl*. It is entirely likely that the same was true of the settlement that occurred within the territories of each of what later became known as "The Five Boroughs", the Danish fortified towns of Leicester, Lincoln, Nottingham, Stamford and Derby.

What distinguished this region in general, however, is the fact that at some unknown point in the earlier tenth century, the five several districts concerned then coalesced into a Danish confederation. By 939 at the latest, this entire region (with the possible exception of southern Rutland (p.12)) – between the Welland and the Humber, and between the south-western Leicestershire boundary of Watling Street and the North Sea – was emerging as a political entity. Invaded and occupied by the hated Hiberno-Norse kings of York and Dublin, and subsequently liberated in 942 by King Eadmund; the Five Boroughs nevertheless continued to retain a unique political identity. As late as 1013 they submitted as a whole to the Danish invader, Sven Forkbeard; and two years after that they acted likewise towards the English Eadmund Ironside.

More than this, the area in question was specifically recognised by King Aethelraed the Unready (or "lacking in counsel"), probably in 997, as a district with institutions of its own that were distinctive even within the wider context of the Danelaw. First, it had its own governing body, the assembly of the Five Boroughs, at which presided the *ealdorman* (the earlier Anglo-Saxon term for a *jarl* or *eorl*) and the king's reeve (a senior executive officer). Below this level, secondly, were the individual meetings of the separate boroughs with some responsibilities also, we may infer, for jurisdiction over each of their adjacent territories: in cases of disputed criminal guilt, for example, proof by ordeal of cold water or of boiling water or of red-hot iron could only take place within a royal borough. At Lincoln, Stamford, and some other Danish centres elsewhere, at least, there is evidence for the existence of 12 "law men" who may have adjudicated at such courts. Thirdly, each borough's dependent territory was subdivided into administrative districts with judicial, military and fiscal functions called wapentakes

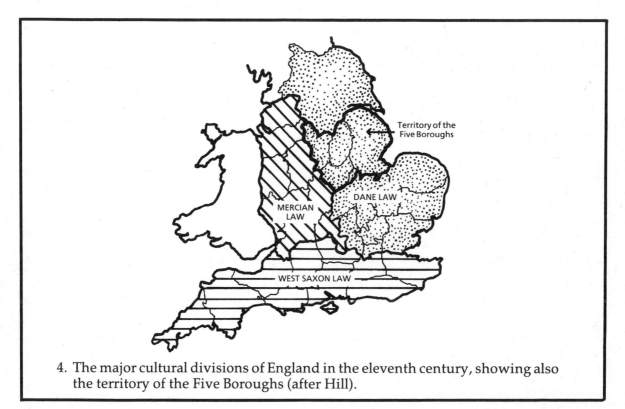

4. The major cultural divisions of England in the eleventh century, showing also the territory of the Five Boroughs (after Hill).

(so named after the flourishing of weapons then taken to mark assent to decisions reached in such public meetings). The business of the wapentake court, which met once every four weeks, was mainly to do with the control of crime – theft and cattle-rustling in particular – and the rounding up of stray beasts; but equally it might testify to the legitimacy of some land- or trade-transactions. In this case the court was attended by the twelve leading thegns (p.22–3) of the wapentake who appear to have been responsible for seizing, and formally accusing, those against whom the reeve wished to take proceedings and, by a unanimous or two-thirds majority vote, for pronouncing judgement on the defendant – a process which is usually taken to mark the origins of the "English" jury-system. Reeve, thegns and all the witnesses had to swear on holy relics placed in their hands which, if perjury was later discovered, might then be amputated, or a large fine paid *in lieu* in proportion to social status. Fourthly, and at a more localised level still, there was the even smaller assembly of the ale-house, a mysterious body which just possibly might be connected with the meetings of those subdivisions of the wapentakes that are later found throughout Five Borough territory, and known as hundreds (units that must be distinguished from the hundreds of the rest of England where they represented the equivalents of wapentakes). Certainly the men of one such hundred were able to give a collective verdict over local tax liability, according to the document that first brings this nevertheless undoubtedly earlier institution to our attention in Leicestershire, *The Leicestershire Survey* of c. 1130. Finally it should be emphasised that the existence of such an elaborate hierarchy of courts in Five Borough territory should not, of course, be taken to imply that all their proceedings were conducted in the detached and socially remote legal manner of today. This was a small-scale, face-to-face society, and resultant disturbances of the peace – even killing – at any of the four assemblies mentioned, incurred appropriately graded monetary fines far in excess of those levied elsewhere in England.

If politically, culturally and institutionally the Five Boroughs were set apart from the rest of England, so too was their system of tax-assessment. As has already been shown (p.3), in this region (outside south-eastern Rutland) the land-unit of rateable value was the carucate, an overall total of which was distributed downwards from the level of each borough territory, *via* the wapentake to each individual vill within it. On the evidence of Domesday Book alone, however, the duodecimal nature of this distribution is not always apparent, so often are vills divided into manors that may even include territories outside the vills concerned (p.12). In northern Rutland, however, an intermediate system of assessment between the wapentake and the vill was declared in Domesday; while in Leicestershire its arrangement may be proved in detail from the archaic evidence fossilised in the later *Leicestershire Survey* of c. 1130. In both cases, it is clear, the small "hundred" described above acted, as it were, as the agency of duodecimal diffusion for tax purposes, sometimes by itself and sometimes in groups. In Leicestershire, such a hundred comprised between 2 to 13 vills or townships – most usually 3 or half a dozen, which might be assessed collectively at, say, 36 or 48 carucates; and when the hundreds were combined into groups, they might be assessed in their turn at 144 carucates – yet another duo-decimal calculation. The tidiness of this system, however, only becomes fully apparent when the later *Leicestershire Survey* is consulted.

The date at which carucation was first imposed on Five Borough territory including northern Rutland, still eludes historians: it is purely the personal view of the writer that this was more probably earlier in the Scandinavian period than the eleventh century as some scholars would prefer. What is clear, however, is that in Leicestershire carucation was imposed on previously hidated territory. In Domesday (and, indeed, in 1002–4), we still learn of the odd hide in the area, though by 1086 it is being given confusing carucate equivalents (i.e. 1 hide = 18 carucates in 3 cases; but 1 hide = 14½ carucates in the case of Melton Mowbray). Whatever the reason for this, the possession of such land can hardly have been disadvantageous to the holder. It is noticeable that in 1086 many of the leading tenants-in-chief held but one such manor (which is often listed prominently after a new wapentake heading) as had

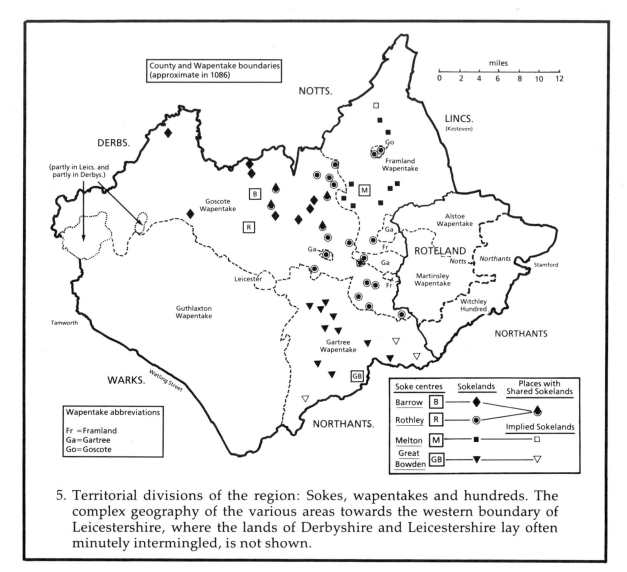

5. Territorial divisions of the region: Sokes, wapentakes and hundreds. The complex geography of the various areas towards the western boundary of Leicestershire, where the lands of Derbyshire and Leicestershire lay often minutely intermingled, is not shown.

their equally important Anglo-Saxon predecessors. It is thus just possible that a distinction is here being made made between units of land that might be legally "conveyed" to others (hides) and units of "taxation" (carucates). Where hides are allotted carucate equivalents, that may simply have been for the purpose of notionally rounding-off the total for the small hundreds concerned: it does not necessarily prove that hidated lands were burdened with a crippling geld assessment. It is equally possible that such lands may have been so privileged – 13 out of 18 of these manors were held in demesne in 1086 – as to have been very lightly taxed or even free of tax altogether, a supposition – it can be no more – that would not have been inconsistent, it may be tentatively proposed, with a known royal policy in the earlier tenth century of encouraging English landholders to take up estates in Scandinavian territory.

If the district of the Five Boroughs could boast distinctive characteristics, it is nevertheless important not to exaggerate the degree of its independence. Over

it, the tenth and early eleventh-century kings may have exercised an uneasy over-lordship, but their sway was acknowledged by the inter-married Anglo-Scandinavian population of the region, and their protection against further Viking invasions was both needed and paid for, at the rate of two shillings per carucate. King Aethelred, moreover, was able to begin his law-code of 997 by declaring that breaches of the "peace" declared personally by himself in Five Borough territory would be beyond any form of atonement "as it best was in the days of his ancestors." The officials who adjudicated at the assembly of the Five Boroughs were English officials: the *ealdormen* (perhaps even the Earl of Mercia or his representative), and not their Scandinavian equivalents, the *jarl* and the *hold*. Two other known dignitaries of the region were described in specifically English terms as "chief thegns" and had been royal "ministers" regularly attending the council of the nation for ten and more years before they were murdered in 1015.

Leicester and the emergence of its county

Ever since the days when Leicester was a Roman city, it must have had a broadly determined territory dependent on it. How far that territory stretched, either then or later, must remain a matter for debate; but that it corresponded in a rough way to the area of the later county is possible. Some shifting of the western boundary, especially where the lands of the later shires of

Leicester and Derby for long lay hopelessly intermingled, and southwards towards Tamworth, is probable; the situation in north-east "Leicestershire", however, is less clear. Whatever the case, the incoming Danes are unlikely to have created a new territory; they more probably took over and perhaps adjusted the area of an old one.

Within this territory there is no need to rehearse the abundant place-name evidence for extensive Scandinavian settlement, though it should be recalled that while such names stretch south-westwards towards Watling Street and even just beyond it, the major concentrations are to be discerned to the north and north-east of Leicester and in the Wreake valley in particular. Many such names clearly reach back to the days when a Danish army or *here* settled itself under the nearby protection of a fortified Leicester. Domesday itself reveals that Leicester Forest was originally called the "wood of the *here*" a term which, by 1086, is taken to include the inhabitants of the whole county.

The formal relationship of Danish Leicester to its district may be measured in three ways, the first of which comprises but a matter of inference. As one of the Five Boroughs, Leicester would of course have had its own courts, but in addition it may also have furnished a *venue* for occasional meetings of the general assembly of the confederation (it could be significant that the only list of these boroughs gives precedence to Leicester followed by Lincoln). It is therefore not without interest that the root of the name "Sanvey" Gate, which lay outside and immediately parallel to the northern defences of the borough (see fig. 21), comprises a Scandinavian word that is more usually found in north-western England but in frequent association with ancient meeting-places. The term is "race-track", and it has been suggested elsewhere that it refers to the sporting-events which, if the Icelandic Sagas are any guide, customarily accompanied the assemblies of Scandinavian peoples.

We are on slightly firmer ground, however, when we turn to two aspects of the political geography of "Leicestershire" which, although largely revealed through Domesday, are unquestionably of pre-Domesday, and probably of pre-eleventh-century origin. The first of these patterns concerns the antiquity of the wapentakes and the boundaries between them. There is much detailed topographical evidence to suggest that these divisions represent a sometimes radical re-adjustment of an earlier pattern of boundaries between areas dominated from centres situated towards the *outskirts* of the later shire territory – the centres of such Sokes as Rothley, Great Bowden and Melton Mowbray (p.18). It may reasonably be postulated that with the fragmentation of the estates of which such Sokes may once have been composed, and the accompanying decrease in the significance of the royal Soke-centres, some reorganisation became necessary. The new system broadly respected the now shunken territories of the Sokes, but the lines now appear to have been firmly drawn to express the dominance of Leicester. The boundaries between the three wapentakes of Goscote, Gartree and Guthlaxton all designedly radiate outwards from the immediate vicinity of Leicester itself, and in a manner that resembles the three Scandinavian "ridings" or "thirdings" of York and Lindsey. The only exception is the wapentake of Framland (fig. 5).

One further spatial measure of the city's superiority over its region in the Scandinavian period may be reconstructed from Domesday Book. In 1086, no fewer than 29 rural places claimed either houses or burgesses (priveleged inhabitants of a borough) appurtenant to them in the town itself (p.46). Rural-urban connections of this kind are more common to the south of Five Borough territory, and for them, three explanations have been preferred. First, these arrangements may reflect a known pre-Conquest practice whereby those granted estates in the surrounding countryside were responsible for the defence and repair of their local fortified centre; secondly, the inhabitants of rural estates may have required places of refuge within urban strongholds; and thirdly, the lords of such estates would have been likely to need both town-houses at which to reside when attending local assemblies, and also urban dependents to deal with the marketing of estate-produce and the purchasing of urban commodities. Clearly none of these explanations is exclusive: a defensive role, for example, is not negated by a commercial function. Yet even when allowance is made for omissions from Domesday, it is striking that if either the refuge or the commercial functions were so crucial, the great majority of Leicestershire's tenants-in-chief (and however inconveniently far from the city they may have had important manors) did not apparently have such urban facilities (p.37–8). What matters here, however, is that all the connected manors listed lay broadcast within, and never beyond, the confines of the emergent shire. The only exception in distributional terms, apart from the lightly populated wooded areas to the west, was that the heart of Framland wapentake was not so linked to Leicester (fig. 6).

With regard to the possible original extent of Leicester's territory before the creation of the shire, the anomalous situation of Framland is at least worthy of remark. Its area to a large extent reflected the earlier territory of the pre-Scandinavian Soke of Melton (p.18), and for the most part that lay quite distinct from the lands of the Sokes of Rothley and Barrow, and, unlike the lands of the Soke of Bowden, far removed from Leicester itself (fig. 5). Framland did not conform to the Leicester-dominated pattern that is so marked a feature of the other wapentakes nor, as we have seen, was its territory densely linked to town-houses in the city. The topography of Framland, moreover, protrudes artificially to the north into what is more naturally the Nottingham-controlled Vale of Belvoir (p.13), while to the south, it adjoins that northern sector of Rutland which emerges in Domesday Book as a detached portion of Nottinghamshire (p.12). In the context of that late emergence of Leicestershire as a county which is now to be described, it is at least curious that two out of a possible three substantial estates in the wapentake that had been forfeited by Earl Morkar (inset 2) were held at farm in 1086 by an ex-sheriff of Nottinghamshire. The possibility that Framland was only added to Leicester territory when the latter became a county cannot be excluded.

The shiring of Five Borough territory could only begin when the confederation ceased to exist. We last hear of the district as a whole in 1015, and even though "Lincolnshire" and "Nottinghamshire" are named as such for the first time in 1016, the relevant entry in the Anglo-Saxon chronicle was written retrospectively, and anyway appears to be contradicted in the former case by the fact that Lindsey is still said to have had its own ealdorman in the same year. The end of the confederation, in fact, is more likely to have followed the accession to the throne in 1017 of the Danish king Knut. It is improbable, however, that the shiring process was accomplished at a stroke. While it may be no more than accidental that "Derbyshire" is first mentioned only in 1049, it is equally true that in Domesday, it emerges as inextricably linked to Nottinghamshire with which it shared the same sheriff and the same shire customs. "Leicestershire" on the other hand only makes its first written appearance in the folios of the Great Survey itself.

The possibly protracted nature of these developments may only be understood against a knowledge of how an Old English shire (a term that means no more than an administrative division) was organised. By this period, and outside the district of the Five Boroughs which, it will be recalled, boasted its own superior assembly, the highest provincial court was that of the shire, at which suit was theoretically owed by all "free" men in the area (p.29–30), and to which

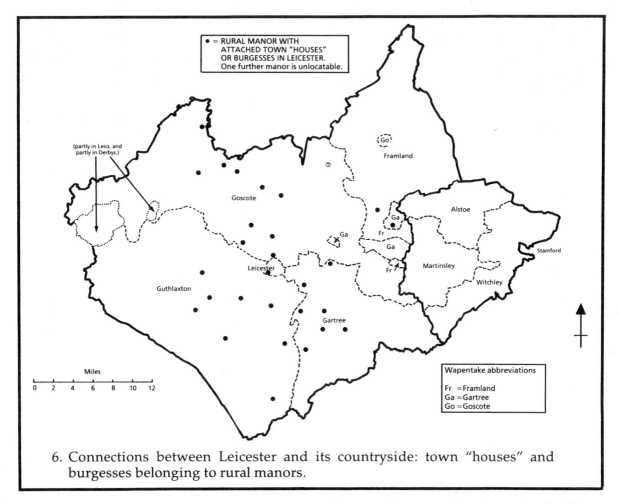

6. Connections between Leicester and its countryside: town "houses" and burgesses belonging to rural manors.

royal directives might be addressed. Below the shire court were the courts of the borough and of the hundred (or, as here, the wapentake). The shire court met twice a year or more frequently if necessary. It was presided over on the one hand by the ealdorman or earl (as he was coming to be called) who, as the direct representative of the king, oversaw the application of the secular law and so took to himself a third of the fines taken under this head (the Earl's "third penny"); the remaining two-thirds being taken by the king. The other co-president of the court was the bishop of the diocese who expounded the ecclesiastical law and oversaw the conduct of oath-taking and, if needful, the ordeals. Also involved was a new type of royal officer or reeve, the shire-reeve or sheriff, whose main duties were executive and financial. It was he who, as the later Latin version of his official title used by the Normans suggests, would eventually act "in place of" (*vice*) the earl (*comes*) – hence the term *vicecomitatus* used in Domesday to describe the "sheriffdom" as opposed to the "county" of Leicester (the latter term being simply descriptive of an area under the control of a count, the nearest social equivalent to an Old English earl that the Normans could imagine).

The transition to this system from that which had operated in Five Borough territory cannot have been straightforward. The general assembly of the confederation had to be dismantled and at least four new shire courts brought into existence, and then supervised by both Earl and Bishop. It is possible that Nottinghamshire may have been covered by the Earl of Northumbria, but the other county-courts would have had to be added to the already heavy load of the Earl of Mercia or his deputies (fig. 13). In the case of bishops, Nottinghamshire lay conveniently within the diocese of York, but both Leicestershire and Lincolnshire were situated a hundred miles away from Dor-

chester-on-Thames in whose diocese they lay. The see was not removed to Lincoln until 1072, six years after the Conquest, and there is no pre-Conquest evidence for the existence of episcopal deputies anywhere in this huge diocese. It is not even entirely clear whether the bishops of Dorchester had any manors in Leicestershire before 1072 (p.19). The probable late emergence of Leicestershire as a fully fledged county, perhaps during the period immediately around the Conquest, could even be indicated finally by the evidence of Domesday itself. There it is recorded that in 1066 the city had answered to the crown only for its *own* customary renders and services; whereas in 1086 it answers for *both* the city *and* the county, unlike Warwick, on the same Domesday circuit but the head of a longer-established shire, which was able to answer for both the borough and the shire for each of these dates.

By 1086, however, the circumstances relating to the governance of the emergent shire have changed. The new see of Lincoln now has a permanent presence in the immediate vicinity of the city (p.46); but the Earls of Mercia are no more. As a portent for the future development of county administration, the increasingly powerful office of sheriff is now already held by the Norman castellan of Leicester, Hugh of Grandmesnil, who also controls two-thirds of the properties in the borough. Hugh may be receiving the "third penny" from the moneyers of the town, but there is no evidence that he, or anyone else, receives the Earl's "third penny" from the profits of justice from the shire. Nevertheless, the shire court is already meeting. There is perhaps a certain timeless irony in the fact that the earliest evidence for this body locally, comes from a single reference in Domesday, where "the shire" is to be found "denying" a claim made about the manor or manors of Thurmaston by no less a person than Hugh of Grandmesnil himself.

Rutland in Domesday Book . . . . T. H. McK. Clough

The historic county of Rutland does not appear as such in Domesday Book. Instead, the main entries for Rutland are divided between Nottinghamshire and Northamptonshire, and are treated in different ways (fig. 5). The northern and western parts of the present county, namely the *wapentakes* of Alstoe (divided into two small hundreds (p.8)) and Martinsley (which together are described as *Roteland* in Domesday), are principally delineated after the main entries of Nottinghamshire, to which county they are attached for tax purposes. In addition, some two-thirds of the entries for Alstoe are repeated under Lincolnshire, with variations in the recorded detail. By contrast the south-eastern part of Rutland, named *Wiceslie* (Witchley) *Hundred*, is to be found amongst the Northamptonshire folios, in which therefore "Rutland" estates are arranged by land-holder rather than geographically. These Domesday divisions differ from the later arrangement of Rutland into five hundreds, though some of the names are preserved.

In a few cases, moreover, settlements outside Rutland answer to manors within it, as Knossington in Leicestershire does to Oakham. Conversely, a few places in Rutland in part at least belong to manors in the adjoining counties. The relationship between Stamford, the nearest of the Five Boroughs, and Rutland, for example, is not entirely clear. Although the town itself was then, as now, mainly in Lincolnshire but with a small portion south of the Welland-crossing in Northamptonshire, there is also reference to a lordship of Portland whose whereabouts remains unknown. Since we also learn that the church of St Peter in Stamford was a daughter church of Hambleton, it is perhaps possible that Portland was effectively in Stamford, but owed allegiance to *Roteland*. This, however, must remain uncertain.

This geographically confused situation is complicated further by the different ways in which land is measured in Rutland. Whereas Alstoe and Martinsley wapentakes in Nottinghamshire are assessed in carucates, Witcheley hundred in Northamptonshire is the only area north of the Welland to be measured in hides. The difference between the duo-decimal system of carucation and the decimal system of hidation adds to the difficulties of fully understanding what these descriptions actually mean. The problem was discussed in detail by F. M. Stenton in *Victoria County History: Rutland* I, who pointed out how uncomfortably Rutland sits on the divide between the geographical uses of these terms. If carucates seem to reflect Danish influence in Alstoe and Martinsley, this may be misleading; for, in contrast to the county of Leicester and the other component parts of the Five Boroughs of the Danelaw,

the place-names of Rutland are predominantly Old English.

These anomalies in the way in which Rutland is described in Domesday Book are undoubtedly due to its historic formation. The origins of the county, which apparently was not fully assimilated into the shire system until the twelfth century, have been the subject of considerable discussion elsewhere. Even so they must remain uncertain. Whatever else can or cannot be learned about Rutland from Domesday Book and other sources of the period, it is certainly clear that its compilers had no reason at all to link Rutland with Leicestershire! *Sic transit gloria mundi!*

The pattern of land-holding in Rutland in 1086 is firmly recorded in Domesday Book. The whole of Martinsley, much of Witchley, and parts of Alstoe were the property of the crown. It is known that before the Conquest in 1066 an area known as *Roteland* (but not the same in extent as the Rutland that had developed by the twelfth century) had been a traditional holding of the queens of Anglo-Saxon England in the tenth and eleventh centuries; further, it can be argued that this land can be identified as a royal Mercian estate in the ninth century. Such royal ownership is enshrined in the naming of the village of Edith Weston after Eadgyth, the wife of Eadward the Confessor, who survived him by 9 years, dying in 1075. Thus Rutland developed into a county as a result of influences entirely different from those which produced its neighbours, including Leicestershire.

Eadward the Confessor had intended that after his death his possessions in Rutland should pass to the Abbey of Westminster, which he had re-founded. However, after Eadgyth's death, William I did not observe Eadward's wishes, but kept the property in his own hands, granting the churches of Oakham and Hambleton to Albert the Clerk. Nevertheless, the claim of the Abbey was still active, and we find that each of the three principal manors in Martinsley, which the king retained, namely Oakham, Hambleton and Ridlington, are described in Domesday Book as *Church soke* (p.23). Eventually, the Abbey was to be granted possession of at least part of the property with which it should have been endowed by William I. In the case of Oakham, this gave rise to the division of the manor into two portions: Deanshold, which included the church, and belonged to the Abbey; and Lordshold, including the castle, which was to be granted by the crown to successive lords of the manor. As a legacy of Norman England, the Dean and Chapter of Westminster still owned property in Oakham until about 50 years ago, and they retain many archives relating to its holdings in Rutland.

2. STRUCTURES OF LANDHOLDING

Introduction . . . . Editor

The main subject of the Domesday investigation was land: who owned it, how much it was worth, and its taxable value. The manner in which these matters were reported, however, is far from simple to unravel at first glance, while the organisation of landholding that lies behind the written record (and which therefore has to be reconstructed from it) is impossible to understand without a long chronological perspective.

In this chapter, therefore, it will be essential first to look back even beyond the Scandinavian period to patterns of landholding that seem to have typified those earlier times in the region; and secondly to examine the ways in which the fragmentation of such patterns over the subsequent centuries is eventually reflected in the presentation and terminology of the Domesday record.

Some Anglo-Saxon multiple estates . . . . Jill Bourne

The evidence of recent work shows that over most of England in the early and mid-Saxon periods there was a considerable degree of regularity in land organisation. The major units of land at this time, although varying in size, were substantial, covering perhaps a hundred square miles or more, each one looking into a royal centre. Each royal administrative unit, known as a *regio*, would have been made up of several subordinate estates as well as land which had not yet been incorporated into a formal tenurial structure. All of these subordinate estates contained a range of resources and each would have been obliged to render a variety of goods and services to the royal centre and to provide for the king and his retainers when they came to the *regio*. It must be remembered that the king and his court were almost constantly on the move, living off the produce brought into the royal centres as they progressed between them. Within the *regio* the subordinate estates would have shared common grazing; evidence for this may be seen perhaps in the detached parts of Gartree Wapentake which have been stranded like islands within Goscote Wapentake (fig. 5).

We know for certain that a system of subordinate 'multiple estates' within *regiones* existed in Kent, Northumbria and early Wales. Although the evidence elsewhere in the country for these estates is less conclusive it is still possible, with care, to piece them together. It is important to remember that the landholding patterns which we are able to recognise from a detailed study of Domesday Book are the outcome of late Anglo-Saxon land organisation and government, which in turn is the result of previous centuries of shifting patterns of land-ownership and of much fighting for overlordship in the earliest English period. The pattern of earlier land-holding has been altered further in Leicestershire as a result of the destruction and changes brought about by the Danish invasions and settlement of the late ninth to early tenth centuries. Some of these changes are readily detected, others less so. Although the evidence of Domesday is crucial in the reconstruction of Anglo-Saxon 'multiple estates' other evidence is essential in order to support that testimony; Domesday alone is not enough. We need the addition of the evidence afforded by archaeology, place-names, ecclesiastical connections, land charters (of which Leicestershire and Rutland unfortunately possess only one each), topography, field-work and the logic of parish boundaries; all are needed to piece together a convincing argument. This is particularly true when attempting to reconstruct non-royal multiple estates which, by the time of Domesday (and almost certainly during the previous two or three centuries) had begun to undergo a process of fission: that is the splitting off from mother estates of parcels of land which were then given as rewards to followers of the King or the nobility, with these parcels, in their turn, sometimes being split further.

In this short section it is possible only to point to a few examples of putative multiple estates in Leicestershire and from here readers must undertake their own detective work. Place-name evidence, for example, would suggest that a group of vills in the south-east of the county could have comprised one such estate. East Langton, West Langton, and Thorpe Langton (fig. 7). Neighbouring Tur Langton is also a daughter chapel of Church Langton and as such must be included in the estate. This latter name incidentally, is not a *lang* (long) *tun* (settlement) as are the others, but contains the personal name *Tyrthel* with the suffix *tun*-Tyrthel's settlement or village. The topography of the area demands that Shangton is also included in this unit of land although there is no other evidence to support its inclusion.

W. G. Hoskins has already drawn our attention to the Domesday estate of Geoffrey Alselin which comprised Billesdon, Rolleston, Goadby, Keythorpe and Hallaton (fig. 8). Given its topographical relationship to the rest of the estate, the latter is rather fittingly named the *tun* in a *halh* (a corner of land). In 1066 this estate had belonged to the Toki whose name is preserved in neighbouring Tugby. Keythorpe is a daughter chapel of Tugby as is East Norton which lies to the south-east of Tugby. As was also the case with Shangton the facts of topography seem to point here to Skeffington having been a component part of this land unit. In order to round off this corner of Toki's estate, Allexton, lying as it does on the Leicestershire-Rutland county boundary, may also need to be included in it although it equally well may have belonged to an estate of which Horninghold once formed a part.

This putative multiple estate demonstrates the main problem which arises when trying to reconstruct these early land units, that is, just what weight should be placed on each fragment of evidence: what is the balance of probabilities? In this instance, for example, although the Eye Brook provides a neat topographical edge to the whole estate we cannot ignore the fact that the boundary between the wapentakes of Gartree and Goscote cut Toki's estate in half from north-west to south-east. Clearly, the exact line of a boundary shifts over the centuries especially when we remember that in the earliest English period the line may well have been only very roughly delimited between one settlement/estate/*regio* and another. However, when a boundary follows the line of a watershed (a topographic feature associated with boundaries of land units) as this one does, it is likely to be ancient. Further work on this estate might provide an answer to this and other similar questions in the county. The ancient saltway which runs north-east/south-west across Framland Wapentake, for example, poses a similar problem. This ancient road follows the line of the watershed from Belvoir right across to Barrow-on-Soar, with the logic of topography again demanding that it should form in this case the county boundary. Instead, we find, lying in the Vale of Belvoir, along its whole length, a row of parishes which quite clearly must once have been part of what is now south-east Nottinghamshire.

Claybrooke Parva which lies next to the Warwickshire border in the south-west of the county was the centre of another putative multiple estate and is the subject of one of the two surviving Leicestershire and Rutland land charters (AD 962). (The other charter relates to Ayston, Rutland (p.16–17)). This estate comprised the nine civil parishes of Claybrooke Magna and Parva, Ullesthorpe, Bittesby, Wigston Parva and part of Sharnford, along with Wibtoft, Willey and Copston which are now in Warwickshire (fig. 9). There is evidence that this riverine estate contained within its boundaries the whole range of agricultural resources, which would have been necessary for self-sufficiency, e.g. woodland, a dairy farm, open pasture, arable and meadow. The whole of this estate may well have been known originally by the name Claybrooke, with the names of the subordinate settlements arising out of a need for identification as a result of the process of fission.

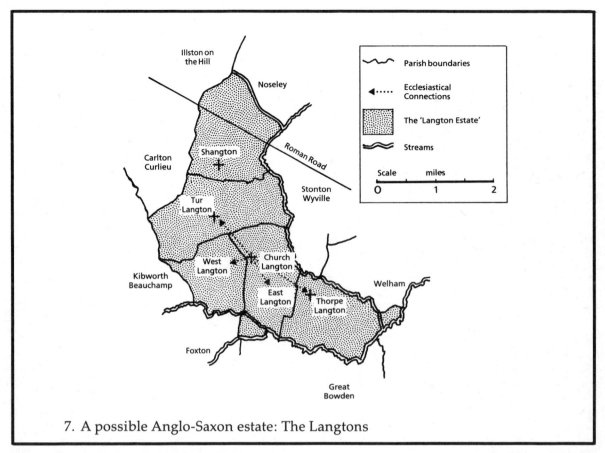

7. A possible Anglo-Saxon estate: The Langtons

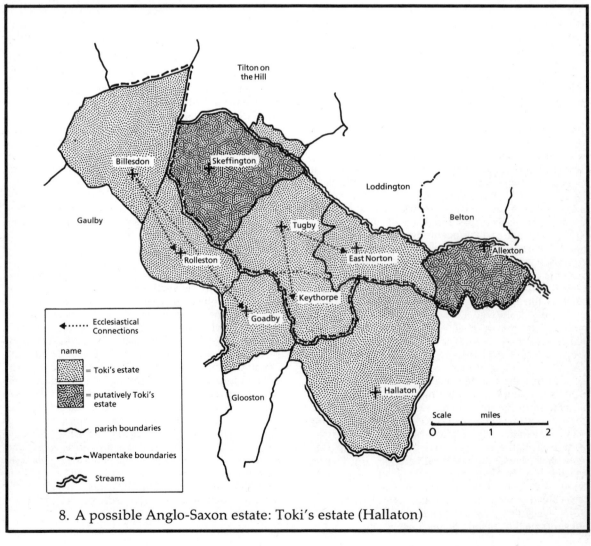

8. A possible Anglo-Saxon estate: Toki's estate (Hallaton)

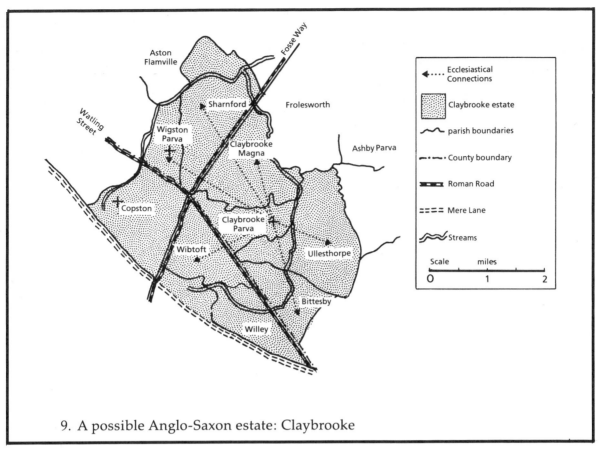

9. A possible Anglo-Saxon estate: Claybrooke

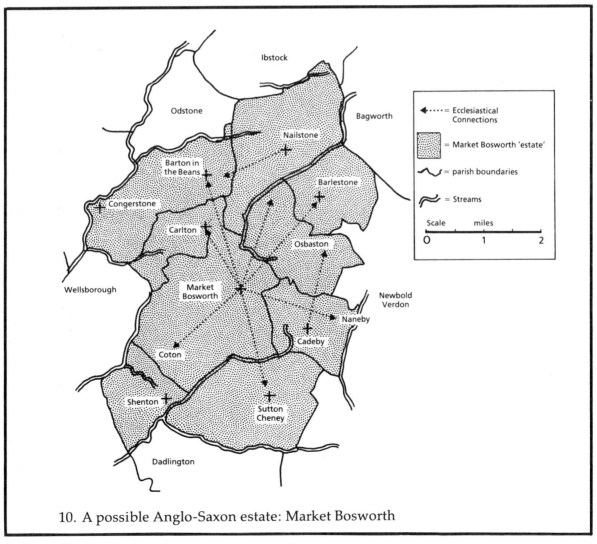

10. A possible Anglo-Saxon estate: Market Bosworth

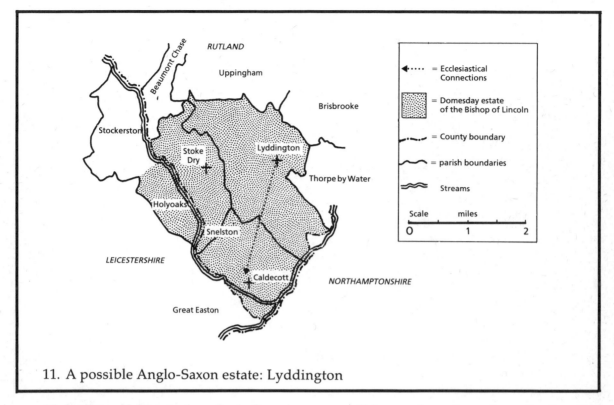

11. A possible Anglo-Saxon estate: Lyddington

Market Bosworth lying twelve miles to the east of Leicester, was once the central place of an estate which comprised at least eleven subordinate settlements. Two of the place-names within this estate indicate the specialist functions they served: Barton is the *bere* (barley) *tun* (settlement); Carlton the *Ceorl's tun* (settlement of the free-men). Figure 10 demonstrates how ecclesiastical links can be used in order to piece together the subordinate members of the estate. Carlton, Coton, Sutton Cheney, Naneby, and Barlestone are all chapelries of Market Bosworth; Nailstone is a chapelry of Barton which in turn is a daughter of Bosworth. Osbaston is divided into East Osbaston which is a chapelry of Bosworth, and West Osbaston which is a chapelry of Cadeby, thus bringing Cadeby into the estate. Again, the topography seems to compel the inclusion of Congerstone in this unit although there is no other evidence which connects it to Bosworth. The place-name Congerstone (King's settlement or farm), is an interesting one in that it must pre-date the Viking invasions, because Danish society was not organised in a way that would have produced the name. Unfortunately we do not know the rôle within Anglo-Saxon estate organisation a place so named would have served.

Moving across to Witchley hundred in Rutland we find recorded in Domesday a small estate centred on Lyddington which was held by the Bishop of Lincoln T.R.W. and by Bardi T.R.E. with *sac* and *soc* (p.22–23). Stoke Dry and Caldecott (which is a daughter chapelry of Lyddington), were members of this estate along with the 'lost' settlement of Snelston, which lay about 1 mile north of Caldecott, and the other lost settlement of Holyoaks which was sited across the Eye Brook, the boundary here between Rutland and Leicestershire. This connection across the Eye Brook must be a reflection of an early stage of English settlement.

In this short section it has been possible only to indicate where five possible early Anglo-Saxon multiple estates might be found. Others are waiting there to be uncovered by the patient researcher who cares to try to weave together those few strands of evidence which have survived to tantalise us.

Lordship and the patterns of estate fragmentation . . . . Editor

Some multiple estates, like that at Lyddington, apparently survived intact even down to the time of Domesday; others, like the Hallaton unit, although somewhat eroded, still remained as recognisable composite estates in 1086. By then, however, and probably in the majority of other cases, the almost complete disintegration of such estates had occurred. The putative estate at Claybrooke had probably begun to fragment well before the Scandinavian occupation. By Domesday, what looks as though it had once been a single unit containing some 9 vills, had fissiperated into eleven separate holdings in the possession of people with many similar fragments of land that were widely dispersed both within Leicestershire and outside it.

It is possible to observe one late example of this centrifugal process in a little detail. In the Domesday folios for *Roteland*, one of three extensive, and still complete, multiple estates forming part of the dower lands of the late Anglo-Saxon queens was Ridlington. Within this estate, and lying between Ridlington itself and Uppingham, was situated a small township that may possibly once have been called "Thornham". By 1046, however, according to a charter of that year, the place had already come into the occupation of a royal thegn called Aethelstan, and by then it was known accordingly by a new name, *Aethelstan's tun* or, as it is spelled today, Ayston. That the re-naming had occurred *before* the place was granted to Aethelstan outright, firmly indicates that previously he had held Ayston on lease in return for military service: in other words, he was occupying what contemporaries described as "thegn-land". A typical first stage in the gradual process of detachment from a larger estate had thus been already accomplished. The second stage, which completed that process, is also illustrated by the charter which Aethelstan received from the king in 1046, for by it, he and his heirs were now granted this little estate in perpetuity. What once had been no more than a component township of the wider Ridlington estate had now been finally converted into a separate "manor" in its own right. And indeed, although Ayston is ignored by name in Domesday (did Aethelstan die without heirs; was he dispossessed?), in visual terms this attractive place still seems to epitomise the classic English manor with its hall, its closely attendant church, and a cluster of tenant-dwellings nearby.

The term "manor", however, must be distinguished at this point from both "township" and "parish", since each represented a distinct form of spatial unit and only in exceptional cases, like that of Ayston, did all three types of unit coincide. Put briefly, a manor was a territorial unit of lordship; a township was a unit of settlement; and a parish was a unit of ecclesiastical organisation. The most basic of these was the township or "vill", as the usual translation of the Domesday latin has it; and it should not be confused with "village" as one modern translation misleadingly terms it (p.34). A township might *contain* a village, a hamlet or detached farmhouses or a number of these in some loose combination, but always within a surrounding area the bounds of which were defined. It was to this secular unit as a whole that the Crown looked for the purposes of tax-*assessment* (p.8) as opposed to its collection, and for the sake of the local enforcement of public order. Parishes on the other hand may be regarded as the ecclesiastical expressions of old multiple estates, of townships or even of the manors that often came to subdivide townships (p.13–16). In the case of Ayston, for example, it is entirely likely that it had lain originally within the wider parish of Ridlington which also then included a number of other vills. It is equally probable that Ayston only became a parish in its own right after the township had become an independent manor and its lord had erected a private church or chapel next to his hall (p.38–40).

What, then, more precisely was a manor? The central meaning of the latin word *manerium* has long been recognised as referring originally to a dwelling, a special residence or, in other words, a lord's hall. And if we ask why that was so, the answer, in theory, is reasonably straightforward. On the one hand, the hall of a lord was the localised collecting-centre for the geld for which the lord was therefore answerable to the Crown; on the other hand, it was to a lord's hall that rents in kind or cash were also rendered to him by his tenants, and suit of court to his "hall-moot" performed by them. (It is usually presumed that such a "court" – to which compulsory attendance was owed by the tenants of the manor – would have restricted its activities to the local supervision of land transmissions between tenants, the labour services owned by them (p.17), the timing of the agricultural routines of the farming year; and to the punishment of misdemeanours too petty to excite the attention of the wapentake court.) If that seems to have been the theory, it cannot have been the universal practice, for clearly some so-called manors could not then boast halls. In human affairs, however, ideals and practice do not necessarily coincide: if need be, taxes could still be collected and courts assembled in the open air, or tenants could be obliged to walk elsewhere. What matters here is that, tax-collection aside, two aspects of lordship were simultaneously involved: the one concerned the lord's rights of possession over

his land; and the other, his jurisdictional rights over his tenants. In Domesday Book, the former concept is constantly expressed in the latin word *terra* – land; the latter idea, but less frequently, by the Old English term *soc* – the right of jurisdiction (in literal terms, the "seeking" of a lord or his court – and hence – the "suit" of court that lords demanded of their tenants).

All the *land* of a classic manor lay in the possession of the lord but he himself occupied only a part of it, the hall and the farmland attached to it, whether that comprised a separate ring-fenced area or land inter-mixed with the ridge and furrow of his tenants. This was the land that Domesday describes as held "in demesne". Beyond or intermingled in that area lay not only the uncultivated woodland and pasture, but also the ridges of his tenants: the "customary land", from which accustomed labour services were owed on the demesne farm and customary payments to the lord in cash or in kind rendered by the tenants. Even woodland might be divided between the lord and his customary tenants: at Rotheley there were "the demesne wood" and "the wood of the villeins" – the inhabitants of the vill. Where manors were far-flung, their outliers took the general name of the manorial grange in each, the berewick or corn-farm. Berewicks were largely, but not wholly, extensions of the demesne. In the whole manor of Oakham, the only demesne ploughs were the two working from the king's hall, yet the manor contained 5 berewicks. The absence of demesne ploughs in these berewicks, however, should not be taken to indicate that the king possessed no demesne land in them. On the contrary, it is clear that he did, but in these places he had no need to provide his own ploughs since the customary tenants would have ploughed his land for him as part of their labour-services. To obtain such services, consequently, each berewick needed to contain customary land as well as demesne land. In the classic manor, therefore, the lord had rights of property in both the demesne land and the land of the dependent peasantry. For the lord's purposes, the two were inextricably linked.

In addition to his rights over land, the lord also possessed seignorial rights over people: rights that were ultimately expressed in the powers of "jurisdiction" he could claim over his dependents, and hence in his ability to hold a court. Put more crudely, a lord thereby gained the right to pocket the fines paid at that court. In the Domesday folios for Leicestershire, the word *soc* by itself is used only when it was necessary to know who received such profits; that is, when the influence of a manorial centre extended over the lands of more than one vill whether these lay adjacent or apart. The *soc* of Ibstock lay in neighbouring Bagworth; the *soc* of Burton-on-the-Wolds belonged to Loughborough some miles away. It is significant that in most such cases, the subordinate vill was held by a sub-tenant of the lord in question. In the case of the vast majority of the classic manors, however, it must be inferred that the right of *soc* was presumed to have lain with each of the lords concerned, and that the profits of jurisdiction were therefore included in the valuation. *Soc* involved payments that were as customary as any other.

It is here than that we must complicate the simplified description just given of the two rights of property and of jurisdiction which the lord of a classic manor *simultaneously* claimed over his customary lands. For in numerous instances the two rights are found to be separable. In such cases some or all of the customary land was *not* owned by the lord of the manor but the rights of *soc* over it were still in his possession. As a result, although the land in question was owned by others, the peasant proprietors of it nevertheless remained within the *soc* of the lord of that land. Land of this kind therefore was called sokeland, and the men who occupied it, sokemen.

To understand how this extraordinary situation may have come about we must look back to the period discussed in the last section. There it was explained how a distinction needs to be drawn between on the one hand the *regiones*, the units of royal administration, and on the other hand, the subject estates – some of them royal – which comprised each such area and which looked into a royal centre for various purposes. For a unit of royal administration was also a unit of royal jurisdiction, a whole territory, in fact, over which the king, not a private individual, had his *soc*. It is not hard to see, therefore, how such an area might become known as a "Soke", to the royal centre of which all the surrounding estates – whether royal or not – would have looked for the purposes of justice and other matters; privileges they would have had to pay for, either in services or in payments to be king. Thereafter, if rights in the *lands* of such estates were granted away by the Crown to privileged individuals, the king nevertheless still reserved to himself in such cases the rights of jurisdiction. It was only later that varying levels of jurisdiction would also have been granted away to individual lords, and with them, the rights to the accompanying services and payments that had formerly been rendered to the Crown (p.22–23). The erosive forces of fission affected not only multiple estates but also whole Sokes.

Four such territories emerge from the Domesday folios for Leicestershire: the still royal Sokes of Rothley and Great Bowden, and the two Sokes of Barrow-on-Soar and Melton Mowbray, both of which were in private hands. By 1086, all of them look like the tattered remnants of what once probably had been more cohesively organised territories. Each had a central manor and each had islands of dependent sokeland lying dispersed and detached over many miles in the areas adjacent to them. Work in progress on the royal Soke of Great Bowden, however, serves to indicate the manner in which the remorseless processes of fission may have led to such patterns. There it may be shown that the royal centre at Bowden probably once dominated an extensive continuous area that embraced perhaps a dozen or so putative multiple estates in a territory stretching northwards almost to the lands of Leicester itself, eastwards towards the Rutland border, and westward as far as Theddingworth on the river Welland. By 1086, and although every one of these multiple estates had by then fragmented, the Crown still retained one or more parcels of royal sokeland (the smallest being no more than 2 bovates) in every one of these former units. Where sokemen are to be found residing on other than royal land in this area, therefore, we must presume that the Crown has granted away its right of *soc* over their lands to the lords either of the new estates, or to some other individual. In other cases, as at Theddingworth, the land itself appears to have been granted away, but the *soc* remained with the Crown.

The probable extent of the original territories of the four great Leicestershire Sokes (conceivably once there may have been no more than three in the area, were Barrow to be regarded as later split from Rothley)

fills the entire map of eastern Leicestershire (fig. 5). Only the western, largely wooded region of the Domesday county lacks such territories even though low densities of sokemen are to be found even there. Whether this was due to the later settlement of this sparsely populated region or, to the possibility that there is at least one ancient, but now lost, Soke-centre still to be discovered there, we cannot tell.

By 1086, therefore, a long drawn-out process of fragmentation had largely, but not quite, destroyed what appears to have been the simpler land-holding and jurisdictional structures of earlier times. On the one hand we may witness the survival or semi-survival of some multiple estates, a very few of which, like those based on Hallaton or Lyddington, could now boast high privileges of jurisdiction in the shape of *sac* and *soc* (p.22–23). Other multiple estates had splintered into classic manors, some of which were coterminous with the lands of their vills, but many of which represented the subdivisions of one vill. In perhaps the most extreme case, the township of Swinford in the southern tip of Leicestershire, the vill was split between 6 tenants-in-chief who shared at least 7, and probably 10, different "manors" between them (though one of these may once have been thegn-land). More complex still, in one of these holdings, a "manor" so minute as to be not worth the name (it had no demesne and contained no customary tenants), a mere 2 bovates were held by one Ulf from one Ralph who, in his turn, held it from the Bishop of Lincoln who, as tenant-in-chief, of course held from the king.

On the other hand there was the widespread incidence of sokeland both in Leicestershire and, outside the royal dower-lands (over which *soc* nevertheless seems to have been recently granted to the church of Westminster) in Rutland. What appear to have been the surviving outlines of earlier territorial entities were, by 1086, in a much depleted condition, eroded both from within and from without. If the head manor of the Soke of Bowden itself had split by the time of Domesday, the sokelands of the Soke of Barrow were becoming manorialised. Within them not only the Earl of Chester, but also 4 of his *milites*, had established demesne lands and the sokemen had shrunk in number to a minority of the peasant population (p.30). Some of the Countess Judith's lands, like Foxton, Gumley and Blaston look as though they have been detached from the parent manor of the Soke of Great Bowden, yet in the first two of these, demesne lands, slaves, and villeins were present while the single inhabitant of her holding at Blaston was a villein. Conversely, some sokelands which had become detached from their parent Sokes had remained unmanorialised: the Countess's 7 demesne "manors" in Guthlaxton wapentake were all innocent of internal demesne-farms and their populations were overwhelmingly dominated by sokemen. In the most extraordinary case of all, at Tolethorpe (Rutland) in 1066, the king was said to have retained the *soc*, but the place was held as a *manor* and held collectively by a group of 8 sokemen! There is nothing uniform or unchanging about the patterns of landholding described in Domesday Book.

3. LORDS AND THE LAND

Landed influence on the eve of the Conquest . . . . Editor

Evidence concerning who actually held land in the region for the period c. 1066–c. 1070 (for that seems

to be what T.R.E. means in Leicestershire at least) is far less easily interpreted than is that for 1086. The earlier owners are often not named. In those cases where an earlier landholder is mentioned, moreover, the absence of further information regarding status or parenthood, for example, makes the reappearance of otherwise suggestive common names difficult to use with confidence: was such an individual, for example, the earl of that famous name, or simply some quite petty landholder? Often it is impossible to tell; though in a few cases a degree of reasonable probability may be accepted. The final problem here, is that there is a good deal of evidence to show that elsewhere, and probably in Leicestershire and Rutland too, the name given as that of the landholder before the Conquest quite possibly was sometimes that of the occupying sub-tenant as opposed to that of the individual who in reality possessed the estate in question. It is only with these cautionary observations in mind that it is possible to outline certain aspects of the territorial power-structure of the pre-Conquest period. Always it must be remembered that the Domesday entries for vast tracts of Leicestershire and, most frustratingly of all, for the overwhelming majority of the extensive estates of the greatest Norman landholder in the shire, Hugh of Grandmesnil, do not include the names of those whom the Domesday scribes called the *antecessores* of the foreign lords who superseded them. It is therefore impossible to reconstruct with any precision the balance of landed influence in the region before 1066.

Two features of the regional pattern, however, are beyond doubt: in Leicestershire, neither the King nor the church could boast extensive land-holdings. There, the traditional core of the royal holding was clearly restricted to two areas: the royal Soke of Bowden in the south; and its equivalent, centred on Rothley, in the north. If these two jurisdictions, with their far-flung and scattered components, might once perhaps have served to dominate what may have been one of the major route-ways running from south to north through Leicester, the fact was that the greater part of the city itself bears all the signs of having been granted away before 1066 to some mighty subject – quite possibly, as was suggested by F. M. Stenton, to a Mercian Earl (p.47). For the rest, the pre-Conquest lands of the Crown in the region were restricted to the extensive estates that lay in the hands of the Confessor's Queen Edith (d. 1075), the real core of whose estates was situated to the east of some scattered holdings in Leicestershire, in what then was known as *Roteland* (p.12).

If the Crown was unusually weak in the region as a whole by this standard, so too was the church which in other districts had long profited from pious donations of land from subject and king alike. In Leicestershire, however, the ecclesiastical estates recorded appear to have been both scattered and largely of recent acquisition. If the origins of the Leicestershire grants made to the Archbishop of York and the one post-Conquest grant made to the Bishop of Durham in Rutland (and hence the implied connection with Northumbria) must remain a mystery; the 16 holdings in Leicestershire and the 2 in Rutland, which are credited to the newly founded Bishopric of Lincoln, seem largely to have been of post-Conquest date though, bearing in mind the problem of prior subtenancies, it is nevertheless a matter for remark that in Leicestershire, both Buckminster and Misterton – the two local place-names that may connote the presence of minsters (p.38) – lay within the bishop's "later" estates; and that another, incontrovertibly early minster-centre at Breedon-on-the-Hill is ignored entirely in Domesday. The only other church holdings in the region were but marginally significant and belonged to the abbeys of Coventry, Peterborough and Crowland to which, in the first two cases, it is known, Leicestershire estates had

been granted less than twenty-five years prior to the Conquest.

In Rutland, the overwhelming domination of the Crown in this tiny area in 1066 is beyond dispute. Where then did landed power lie in Leicestershire at this time? The answer to this question depends in part on how we view the later holding of the county's leading Norman figure, Hugh of Grandmesnil, who, for all we know, may have stepped into the shoes of some powerful Anglo-Saxon predecessor who is simply not named amongst Hugh's *antecessores* in Domesday. It has recently been implied, for example, that Hugh's *antecessor* in some of his Warwickshire lands as well as some of those in Gloucestershire, Oxfordshire, Northamptonshire and Leicestershire may have been one Baldwin son of that Herlwin who had been an important figure in the west midlands in the reign of Knut. The only Baldwin to be mentioned in all 74 of Hugh's Leicestershire manors, however, is an unidentifiable Baldwin who *together with* one Aelfwine held a mere half of one vill T.R.E. – a manor which Hugh himself later did not even hold in demesne, as opposed to subinfeudating it to one of his followers. It is possible, in fact, that Hugh's holding was made up of two elements: a hard core of lands that came to him from some previously important person's estate, and a hastily contrived *mélange* of further lands that had been gathered together from other sources. Some of the latter are easily identified: they included manors once held by such influential personages as Queen Edith, Earl Ralph of Hereford (d. 1057), and the disgraced Earl Waltheof; as well as estates formerly in the hands of a few more modest, and hence, less easily identifiable figures; while one of Hugh's manors, Thurcaston, had simply come to him as the outcome of a negotiated exchange between the king and another Norman tenant-in-chief (p.26).

If these impressions are correct, to identify the un-named *antecessor* of the large core of Hugh's estates, we must look elsewhere for a figure whose existence might even have been taken for granted by the Domesday Comissioners. In seeking a possible solution to this problem, two related factors cannot be ignored. First, he who dominated Leicester, whether before or after the Conquest, clearly also dominated the evolving shire around it. Secondly, there is evidence enough, even from fiefs other than that of Hugh of Grandmesnil, to suggest that one family above all, one of the greatest in the realm – a family powerful enough to act as a Midlands counterweight to the ever expanding influence of the house of Godwine in the south – had once possessed, even on the fragmentary evidence of Domesday, a decisive stake in the territorial disposition of Leicestershire. That family was the house of Leofric, Earl of Mercia from *c.* 1023 to 1057, whose son then succeeded to the earldom, and whose youthful grandson Eadwine in his turn took over the earldom in *c.* 1062 and remained technically in possession of it, following his submission to William, until his murder in 1071 (for the family connections, see inset 2). Even in 1086, it is still possible to trace some 200 carucates in the shire which may have belonged at one time or another to the house of Leofric, while it would have been a matter for remark indeed had Leicester itself not been in the hands of a Mercian Earl before 1066. Only a year before the Conquest, we receive a strong hint from *The Anglo-Saxon Chronicle* that Leicestershire was firmly part of Eadwine's Mercian earldom, for in 1065 when his younger brother Morkar was chosen by the Northumbrians in place of their previous ruler Tosti (who, it has even been tentatively suggested, may then also have been Earl of Lincolnshire), support for Morkar was specifically raised in Lincolnshire itself and in Nottinghamshire and Derbyshire, but not in the only remaining Five Borough county, Leicestershire. Yet Eadwine, who now joined with his brother, brought with him "men from his earldom", and together they ravaged Northamptonshire and other neighbouring shires which certainly cannot have included Leicestershire. Is it possible, then, that of all the north-central Midlands counties, Leicestershire alone was not implicated in this rising? Was it also simply coincidence that when, in 1068, a rebellion in the north occasioned by the departure of both Eadwine and Morkar from the Conqueror's court was met by William, he appears to have begun his campaign by striking decisively through house-of-Leofric country beginning with the construction of a castle at Warwick, an operation he may have repeated at Leicester, but certainly at Nottingham?

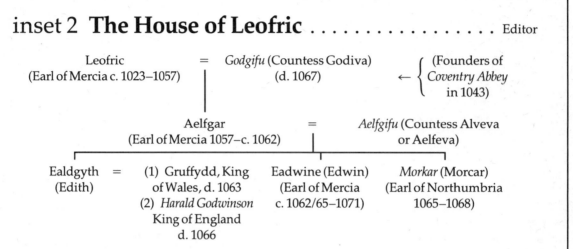

inset 2 The House of Leofric . . . . Editor

Leofric = *Godgifu* (Countess Godiva) ← { (Founders of *Coventry Abbey* in 1043)
(Earl of Mercia c. 1023–1057)   (d. 1067)

Aelfgar = *Aelfgifu* (Countess Alveva or Aelfeva)
(Earl of Mercia 1057–c. 1062)

Ealdgyth = (1) Gruffydd, King of Wales, d. 1063   Eadwine (Edwin)   *Morkar* (Morcar)
(Edith)   (2) *Harald Godwinson* King of England d. 1066   (Earl of Mercia c. 1062/65–1071)   (Earl of Northumbria 1065–1068)

12. Family Tree of the House of Leofric. Popular spellings given in brackets. Domesday landholders in Leicestershire underlined.

The house of Leofric took on a national significance as the power of the family expanded, during the first half of the eleventh century, from its earlier restricted territorial base in the west Midlands (where its strength and its links with Wales long continued) into a major political counterweight to the ever-growing pretensions of the house of Godwin in the south, a rivalry that was ended first by a marriage-alliance with Harald Godwinson (family tree) and secondly by his death at Hastings shortly after.

The influence of the house of Leofric lay in its claim to furnish virtually hereditary Earls for a greater Mercia which, from the time of Leofric onwards, may well have included all or most of the former territory of the Five Boroughs (fig. 13). By 1065, if not before, the then youthful Eadwine had succeeded to the Earldom of Mercia only to find that with the north-east in rebellion against its own unpopular earl, (Harald's brother, Tosti), his own younger brother Morkar was now acclaimed as internal, as opposed to royal, candidate for the Earldom of Northumbria. With the prospect of virtually half of England at their bidding, the two brothers now, and thereafter, acted in concert. Morkar marched his Northumbrians south through Lincolnshire and raised support in the shires of Derby, Nottingham and Lincoln; while Eadwine with "men from his earldom" (which must have included Leicestershire at this time) and many Welshmen joined him at Northampton, in the countryside around which the northerners slaughtered men, burnt houses and corn, and carried off thousands of livestock. If King Eadward was thereby forced to accede to Morkar's popular elevation to the Earldom of Northumbria, the events of 1065 demonstrate that the south-eastern boundary of the territory under the house of Leofric was now unambiguously demarcated by the Welland valley.

In the following year, the two brothers together twice defended this territory – in one chronicle it is called "their earldom"; successfully against the depredations in northern Lindsey of the deposed Earl Tosti, and heroically but disastrously against the combined forces of Harald of Norway and Tosti at the battle of Fulford, close by York. If the weakened forces of the invaders were themselves in their turn decisively defeated (and so left leaderless) by Harald of England at the subsequent battle of Stamford Bridge a few days later, the forced march that then followed, down to London and eventually to Hastings, occurred too soon for Eadwine and Morkar either to regroup their shattered troops or to raise more men in time to join it. With the death of Harald and many of the leading Anglo-Saxon nobility at the battle of Hastings, therefore, Eadwine and Morkar alone were suddenly left as the natural foci of secular political leadership in the English nation; the only possible Anglo-Saxon candidate with any pretension to the English throne – and now elected – being but a boy.

Resistance from London, however, was indecisive as William harried punitively along the Thames to the west of the capital; and perhaps because of this devastating demonstration, both the Earls and the young prince submitted to him.

Their potential danger to the new king, however, continued to be recognised after his coronation. When William returned briefly in triumph to his Duchy in Normandy in 1067 he took the earls, the young prince and other notables with him "in honourable captivity". At some time during the ensuing twelve months, however, William made a statesmanlike peace with Earl Eadwine "granting him authority over his brother and almost a third of England" – presumably greater Mercia – and "promised to give him his daughter in marriage". Jilted, for political reasons, in a match which the handsome and popular young Eadwine had very much desired; in 1068 he and his brother slipped away from court apparently to ally themselves to a new Northumbrian resistance movement centred on York. The precise nature of this connection is not apparant, but the vulnerability of Mercia which lay as a buffer-zone between Northumbria and a vengeful William now approaching from the south was soon to become all too clear. William moved in deadly earnest on Eadwine's borough of Warwick – the key fortified centre for the shire – in which a castle was rapidly thrown up and then placed under Henry Beaumont, the brother of the Domesday Leicestershire's Count of Meulan. This in itself was enough to force Eadwine and Morkar to submit, though never again to be trusted by the Conqueror who now marched directly on Nottingham (it is often argued *via* Leicester), where the subjugation of the borough and the construction of another castle, probably with forced English labour, is said to have frightened the York rebels themselves into abject submission.

13. The Earldoms in 1065. There is a little evidence to suggest that the predecessor of Earl Morkar in Northumbria had some influence in Nottinghamshire (after Hill).

Discredited not only to the south but also to the north (where resistance resurfaced under other leadership in 1069 and 1070 with Danish support), the brothers Eadwine and Morkar fatefully split-up. In 1071, Morkar seems to have sought refuge with Hereward the Wake on what then actually was the Isle of Ely, only to be tricked, it would appear, into what he took to be an honourable submission to William, and then – as one too dangerous to be left at liberty – "flung into fetters without any open charge, and kept in prison to the end of his days." Eadwine, meanwhile, sought every means with which to retaliate by seeking help not only from the English but also from the Welsh and the Scots. Betrayed to the Normans by his own servants, he and 20 of his horsemen died fighting desperately.

Courageous and honourable; generous to the clergy and just sufficiently pious; widely popular, incomparably good-looking, and of renowned lineage; Earl Eadwine may stand as a last symbol of the Old English land-holding society which the Normans so successfully displaced. Even King William, we are told by a biased source, was moved to tears at the news of the treachery that had led to Eadwine's death, "and when the traitors brought the head of their master to him, hoping for reward, he angrily commanded them to leave the country." Eadwine thus became part of legend, an early example of that typically English reaction to glorious defeat. The truth was that, given the advantages open to him through birth and opportunity, he was simply out-calculated by a superior political realist. Immature vigour may make for heroes, but not necessarily for heroes that emerge victorious.

There can be no certain answer to such questions. Eadwine, as in the cases of the great majority of Hugh de Grandmesnil's *antecessores*, is not even mentioned in the Leicestershire section of Domesday; but, equally, he may also have received less than his appropriate territorial due elsewhere in the country. All that might be claimed here is that what once had been seemingly an important comital holding in the shire, the Soke of Barrow-on-Soar, was probably passed on as dower land – *via* the second marriage of Earl Eadwine's sister, Ealdgyth – to no less a person than King Harald himself. The continuing connection between not only the territory of Rutland, but also that of Leicestershire, with actual or potential Queens of Anglo-Saxon England, is therefore not without interest.

Whoever may have dominated Leicestershire as the last undisputed king of the Old English state lay dying, ironically it is somewhat easier to delineate broadly the successively descending levels of landholding from and below that of a Mercian Earl, and in a way which – as the previous chapter implied – also serves to indicate the ever more inferior ranks of lordship that characterised noble status in pre-Conquest society. To do so it will be best to narrow-in on the region from the outside. Clearly it would be misleading to treat the local pattern of landholding in isolation.

Two widely embracing levels of landholding should be noted. There were, first, the scattered estates in the region that belonged to the more extensive holdings of national figures (apart from the house of Leofric) and especially those that belonged to earls: Ralph, Earl of Herefordshire and Oxfordshire (1053–57), a half-French nephew of the Confessor; and Waltheof (from 1067–1076, Earl of the shires of Northampton, Huntingdon, Bedford and Cambridge, and later of Northumbria), who married the Conqueror's niece, the Countess Judith, in *c.* 1072. Unimpressive as the extent of such estates sometimes may have been, their disposition may nevertheless be significant; for the city of Leicester was half-girdled by the lands of the great. Part of Aylestone was held by the widow of Earl Aelfgar of Mercia; most of Wigston Magna and of Stoughton, by Earl Ralph; and most of Oadby certainly, as a well as part of the south-fields area of the borough, and 28 houses within it, probably, by Earl Waltheof. Apart from the post-Conquest estates belonging to the see of Lincoln on the eastern outskirts of the borough and in Knighton, it is worth noting that most of the rest of the lands around the town – at for example, Evington, Belgrave, Birstall or Bromkinsthorpe – were held by one or more unnamed *antecessor* of Hugh of Grandmesnil himself, and may thus also have belonged to major political figures earlier. All of these manors seem to have been held in demesne, while Wigston, Stoughton, Belgrave, Birstall and Bromkinsthorpe also had houses attached to them in the borough (p.xx). It may be added that both Earl Morkar and perhaps Earl Waltheof of Northampton (before the Countess Judith) had held similar Rutland manors in the vicinity of Stamford.

Below this comital level, secondly, were those estates that belonged to men of the next lower social rank. These were they who might have described themselves as king's thegns with a seat in his hall and a place on his council: men who, in days not long gone, might also have described themselves as "chief thegns" in the territory of the Five Boroughs; men whose holdings in a restricted region could sometimes almost rival those of an earl. In our area, such men would have included the Scandinavian-named Toki, son of Auti, who seems to have given his name to Tugby (*Toki's by*); whose estate at "Hallaton" has already received attention (p.13); and whose lands were concentrated in Lincolnshire, Nottinghamshire, Derbyshire and Leicestershire as well as in two other Danelaw districts, Yorkshire and Northamptonshire. Others of his social kind may represent the heirs of those who, at a much earlier period (p.9), had perhaps been encouraged to take up land in Danelaw territory: such men as the English Hearding who held land in Warwickshire as well as in Leicestershire, or the equally English Leofric, son of that Leofwine whose estates had also stretched from neighbouring Warwickshire into our area. Indeed, there is much to be said for the possibility that by 1066–70, the Leofric in question dominated the wapentake of Framland (he may even be the Leofric who held the now deserted *Alestorp* not far over the Leicestershire boundary into Rutland). It would be odd indeed were the Leofric son of Leofwine who, in 1066, owned the Soke of Melton Mowbray and therefore its sokeland at Stathern, not also the same "Leofric" whose paternity is not recorded, but who held the other part of the same vill with *sac* and *soc* in the same year. This "second" Leofric, moreover, may be identified as a "thegn" with status enough to hold a number of other holdings not least in Bottesford, to which the *sac* and *soc* of Stathern belonged.

For the possession of *sac* and *soc* represented a high privilege. We have already seen how the word *soc* might be used at both a manorial level and a district level: what must now be confessed, however, is that historians have so far been unable to decide whether *soc* by itself was the exact equivalent of *sac* and *soc*. If *soc* meant "suit" to a court, then *sac* meant no more than "a cause at law – a matter in dispute", the very reasons why a suitor might wish to come to a court anyway! Nevertheless, the Domesday survey for Derbyshire and Nottinghamshire, for example, regarded the possession of *sac* and *soc* as sufficiently important as to merit a separate list of people (including Toki, who also held his "Hallaton" estate with *sac* and *soc*) who claimed it as their privilege. One explanation for this difficulty would be that the word *soc* was probably taken to refer to the whole gamut of jurisdictional rights from the modest to the considerable. When applied to a manor, *soc* might mean one thing; when applied to a territorial Soke under the control of the king, it surely meant another. With *sac* and *soc*, those weightier matters for jurisdiction that might normally be ascribed to the jurisdictional powers of the court of a royal territorial Soke, are also clearly involved. Both the court of the territorial Soke and any court held by the possessor of *sac* and *soc*, were probably equivalent in their jurisdictional range to the court of the wapentake, where royal, as opposed to seignorial, justice was meted out. It would have been these courts, rather than the wapentake court therefore, that the tenants of such lords probably would have been expected to attend. (If they did attend the wapentake court, however, any fines they may have paid would have been passed to the holder of *sac* and *soc*.) In Leicestershire no more than 19 lords were credited with this privilege, to which total should be added the holder of the Soke of Barrow.

Nine of these lords are said also to have held certain of their lands "freely": each could "go where he would". In this society all men and all land had to be under some lord, the greatest men looking only to the king. At the level of rank under discussion, however, there was a band of society in which men had the freedom to choose particular lords to whom they might wish to attach themselves and some part of their estates. Such men could "commend" themselves and their land to one or more powerful lords of their choice in return for his or their protection or influence. Equally they reserved the right to "recede" with their land from such a lord if they so chose. This right reached down to quite humble levels: at Scalford, for example, 11 carucates had been divided between 5 unnamed and probably unimportant thegns who held the land freely. Those *named* elsewhere, however, were clearly men of at least some local standing although not always extensive landholders, and if we add their number to those holding *sac* and *soc*, we achieve a minimal total of 42 privileged landholders in the shire at the time of the Conquest from amongst whose number, we may guess,

would have been drawn the thegns who made up the wapentake juries.

A thegn was one who "served" a lord either militarily, administratively or even in other capacities: priests might be "altar-thegns", perhaps like the three who held of the King's Alms in Leicestershire, at least one of whom had probably served, as literate clerics did, in the royal administration. Those thegns who did not hold their land freely were therefore tied more closely to their lords than those who did. In either case, however, the extent of land held by a thegn varied markedly. In Nottinghamshire and Derbyshire, the shire customs differentiated between those thegns who held more than 6 manors, and those who held fewer – a distinction which may have been sustained in other areas where duo-decimal calculation was the norm. The Leicestershire evidence in any case is not sufficiently extensive as to allow us to calculate the social distribution of manors T.R.E. All that may be said is that it was occasionally possible for those who described themselves not as thegns, but as free men, to hold far more land than most thegns. Aethelric son of Maergeat, for example, held 9 manors in Leicestershire and other lands in Lincolnshire and Northamptonshire, but in Domesday, it is said, "he was a free man"; whether or not he was also a thegn, we are not told. At the other extreme there were many lowly thegns, some of whom had been placed by their lords in groups of 3 or 5 on a single manor – as at Gumley, Swinford, Loughborough or Scalford – with holdings of only 3 or 4 carucates. It is curious to note that if the central estates of great earls markedly clustered around the city, men at the lowest end of the scale of Anglo-Saxon lordship, whose functions may have been largely military, seem often to have been granted lands on or towards the county boundary.

Domesday Book and the feudal aristocracy of Norman England . . . . Daniel Williams

In a seminal article written almost a century ago, Horace Round concluded that the most novel consequence of the Conquest was the introduction of feudalism into England. Apart from the modification of Round's somewhat legalistic term, "feudalism" to the more sociological and appropriate concept of "feudal society", the essential truth of his hypothesis has never been convincingly challenged. The Normans brought with them the still evolving continental practice of tenure by knight service (a system by which land was held in return for the provision of skilled cavalry-warriors) within an essentially aristocratic hierarchy of overlord, tenant-in-chief and vassal. It was an intrinsically military structure that with certain modifications was well suited to William I's problem of subduing and holding down a hostile subject population. The quasi-military structure of Anglo-Danish England in the eleventh century greatly facilitated the transition to feudal society as the synonymous usage of the terms thegn, knight, vassal, and liegeman of the early post-Conquest charters reveals. Beyond this fact, the debate concerning the nature of the military, quasi-feudal structure of Anglo-Saxon England has proved to be a somewhat arid one which cannot detract from the essential truth of Round's conclusions.

In this area of historical investigation the evidence of the Domesday Survey is vitally important. In the case of Leicestershire, the records of Domesday Book and the later 1130 *Leicestershire Survey* used in conjunction, reveal an almost uniquely detailed picture of one of the greatest upheavals in land ownership in English history. They show the county as it was during

the period of transition between the Conquest itself and the completion of its most important stages in the reign of Henry I (*c.* 1130). In particular, the evidence demonstrates the process by which the castlery of Leicester and the lands under the jurisdiction of its first castellan, which had been given and held *per gladium* (by the sword) as a result of the stormy events of 1068–9, became the early twelfth century Earldom of Leicester.

The substitution of a French for an Anglo-Saxon arsitocracy in the Midlands, as elsewhere, was to be a *de facto* and drawn-out process due to a number of complications that resulted from the submission of three Anglo-Saxon earls: Eadwine of Mercia, Morkar of Northumbria and Waltheof of Northampton-Huntingdon. The immediate consequence of William's unsuccessful attempts to appease his Wessex kinsmen was that effective control of his new kingdom was exercised directly only over the South and the Home counties. The treachery and rebellion of all three earls at various times during the next decade meant that William had to take direct military control of the Midlands and the North. He did this during the rapid and definitive campaigns of 1068 and 1069–70, in the first of which his army moved through Warwickshire, Leicestershire and Nottinghamshire, on its route to York where revolt was suppressed; and in the second of which, he returned to a still rebellious North where he devastated the Northumbrian lands between York and Durham. At that point he marched south-west across the Pennines in winter to occupy Chester and then, to complete his occupation of the Midlands and the Welsh Border, by moving through Stafford,

Shrewsbury, Gloucester and Hereford; disbanding his army eventually at Salisbury on the completion of his victorious and successful circuit. In each of these newly occupied shires he appointed trusted castellans who built and garrisoned castles. In the marcher regions of the North and the Welsh Borders he established palatine earldoms, enfeoffed with his senior commanders like Hugh of Avranches, Roger of Montgomery, William Fitz-Osbern and Robert of Mowbray, men who were not only Norman lords, but also members of the tightly-knit kinship group that constituted the Norman ducal dynasty. Within this most trusted defensive circle, the King appointed lesser men as sheriffs and castellans of the Midland shires. Simon of Senlis eventually received Northampton; Henry of Beaumont, Count of Meulan (who is the distinguished exception to the category of lesser men) received Warwick. According to the chronicler, Orderic Vitalis, Walter "called" Giffard was given Buckingham, the Breton Ralph of Gael, Norfolk; William of Ferrers was given Derby which was held from his castle at Tutbury in Staffordshire, and Hugh of Grandmesnil was appointed castellan of Leicester. Within this two-tier military and feudal regional structure, further *ad hoc* feudal Honors were established over the next thirty years to complete the middle rank of tenants-in-chief by knight service – who also of course included the holders of the great bishoprics and abbacies of Norman England. Such men held their lands from the king by a somewhat capricious allotment of what became known as *servitium debitum* (literally, "service owed") of fully and expensively equipped and trained mounted knights. It was these middling land-holders who completed the feudal and tenurial hierarchy of Norman England which could thus supply a force of some 4,000 knights as the invincible striking force of the royal army. This is the great upheaval in landownership and restructuring recorded in the 1086 Domesday Survey that was then still in the process of being worked out, but which, by the time of the *Leicestershire Survey* of 1130, was virtually completed.

The Norman Honours reflected in the lists of shire tenants-in-chief in Domesday Book, vary enormously in size. They range from the great palatine Earldoms in Fee to the relatively minor, largely Northamptonshire Honour of Chokes consisting of about thirteen knights fees mostly of single manors held by *Gunfrid of Chocques*, a French knight from the town of Chocques, which at that time lay within the county of Hainault.

In return for his modest Honour which included the South Leicestershire manor of Mowsley, Gunfrid owed the King the service of 15 knights. With himself and his brother Sigar included, this total corresponds almost exactly to the number of knights fees that make up the Honour. At this level, like the senior group of the Conqueror's greatest feudal lords, the knights of the Chokes Fee may also have been in fact a close-knit kinship and *conrois* group. In his return to Henry II's *Cartae Baronum* survey of 1166 the Archbishop of York explains '. . . our predecessors enfeoffed more knights than they owed to the king and they did this, not for the necessities of the royal service, but because they wished to provide for their relatives and servants.'

The 'military' knights most probably included the *milites* recorded in Domesday as well as the men of substance recorded as vassals and subtenants. In Leicestershire this group varies from the castellan himself, Hugh of Grandmesnil, who appears as vassal of the widowed Countess Judith, to unidentifiable vassals with Anglo-Saxon names who may be de-classed thegns. The only common factor was the rigorous training, fitness and military skill required of a heavy cavalry warrior during the eleventh century. These subtenants or vassals are in the majority of cases

difficult to pin down. In some instances this is possible. Take, for example, the subtenants of the extensive fee of William of Peverel recorded in the Leicestershire entry. The Honour of Peverel extended over at least half a dozen counties, but lay chiefly in Nottinghamshire, Derbyshire, Oxfordshire and Buckinghamshire. His three named Leicestershire tenants varied from the humble Riculf who held the manor of Kirby Muxloe only, to Payen or Pagen who held, in addition to Lubbesthorpe, manors in Nottinghamshire (Basford), Northampton (Barby) and Buckinghamshire (Tetchwick). The third, Saxfrid of Ashby Magna, who held, in addition to Ashby, manors in Nottinghamshire and Northamptonshire, was the founder of an important vavassour family from which the Northamptonshire and Warwickshire Catesbys claimed descent.

William Peverel could also count amongst his vassals important tenants-in-chief like William Ferrers whose descendent Robert was created Earl of Derby in 1138, and Robert, Despensor (or Bursar) to the Norman earls of Chester. Conversly, Peverel was a vassal of Gilbert of Ghent in Husbands Bosworth. It was a highly complex tenurial situation that defies any attempt at rational explanation. Equally, the Peverel example shows that the Honours with very few exceptions were *ultra comitatum*: transcending shire boundaries, and forming stable loyalties and connections, that were to endure throughout the medieval period. They were in structure and organisation 'little kingdoms'; microcosms of the feudal state with their own courts and officials. Men like the descendents of Robert Despensor, hereditary Bursars or Despensors of the earls of Chester, were typical of the recognisable class of 'Barons of the Fee'; the men of wealth and standing, 'occupying land who were of any account over all England, no matter whose vassals they might be' who, according to the *Anglo-Saxon Chronicle*, swore fealty to the Norman royal dynasty at Salisbury in 1086.

Accordingly, the majority of the recorded landowners of Leicestershire in the Domesday Survey, including vassals like Robert of Burdet and Hugh of Widville whose dynasties were to make their mark upon both the history of the county and the nation, were men of considerable wealth and substance. They were also Frenchmen rather than only from Normandy. A brief examination of the Domesday "List of Landholders in Leicestershire", shows the wide geographical origins of the Conqueror's companions, ranging right across Northern and Western France (fig. 14). Their families were substantial landowners on both sides of the Channel. This new-found wealth was to be directed, not only to the building of cathedrals, abbeys and churches in the austere Romanesque style known to us as Norman, and still to be seen in East Leicestershire and Rutland churches, but also towards the establishment and stocking of forests, chases and parks to fulfil their fervent passion for the violent and dangerous hunting pursuits of their class. This leisure activity and essential training for mounted combat, was to leave its indelible mark upon the topography of Leicestershire and the rest of the kingdom. In the short term it was to mean a further burden upon their Anglo-Saxon tenants and peasants. Orderic Vitalis was to comment upon the brutal Hugh of Avranches, Earl of Chester, a considerable landowner in Leicestershire whose manors included the eastern portions of Charnwood Forest; 'his hunting was a daily devastation of his lands, he thought more highly of fowlers and hunters than husbandmen or monks'. The Anglo-Saxon Chronicle records in verse the hunting enthusiasm of the Conqueror himself and its consequences:

He set apart a vast deer preserve and
*   imposed laws concerning it.*
Whoever slew a hart or a hind

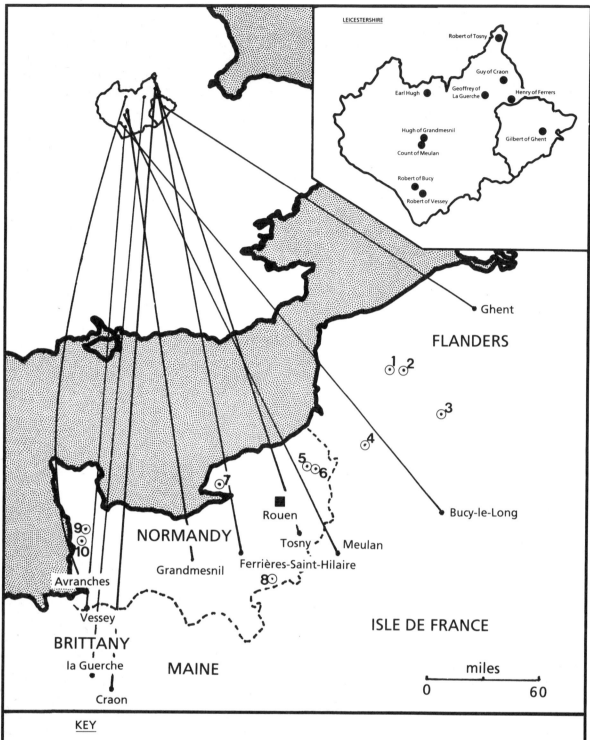

KEY

1. Chocques

2. La Beuvrière

3. Cambrai

4. Picquigny

5. Bully-en-Brai

6. Mortemer

7. Graville-Sainte-Honorine

8. Gouville

9. Saint-Martin-d Aubigny

10. Coutances

14. Origins of the Conquerors

The map shows the continental origins of leading landholders in Leicester-shire and Rutland. The situation in the region of only the more important of their demesne manors is also indicated. Apart from Hugh of Grandmesnil (Leicester), Robert of Tosny (Belvoir) and probably Geoffrey Alselin (Halla-ton), it is not known which of these tenants-in-chief may have had residences in the area in the eleventh century: for most of them the centres for their far-flung estates lay outside it. (For the distribution of castles see Figure 15.)

Was to be blinded.
He forbade the killing of boars
Even as the killing of harts.
For he loved the stags so dearly
As though he had been their father.
Hares also, he decreed should go unmolested.
The rich complained and the poor lamented.

This love of the chase that was to cost the lives of two of the Conqueror's sons, permeated the ranks of the new feudal aristocracy from the King downwards. A close examination of the areas of woodland and waste recorded in the Domesday Survey for the north-west quadrant of the county, reveals that the concentrations of forest (a designation technically only applied to Royal Forests as defined in the draconian new Forest Law alluded to in the above passage from the *Anglo-Saxon Chronicle*), chases and deer parks discernible from medieval documents, are already in existence.

It is highly signficant that the returns of the crown lands for Rothley, on the edge of the Charnwood area, distinguished between the villagers' woodland and the far more extensive lord's woodland '1 league long and ½ league wide'. The woodlands of some of the larger Norman landowners of the Domesday shire, support this afforestation hypothesis in greater detail when comparison is made with later medieval records. The woodland of the Sheriffdom of Leicester – the sheriff being the castellan, Hugh of Grandmesnil – called 'Hereswode', and one of the most extensive afforested areas in the whole county ('4 leagues in length and 1 league in width'), is clearly the nucleus of the Leicester Forest found in later documents. If we add to this the woodland also held by Hugh in the adjacent manors of Anstey (1 league by ½ league with *alia silva* – other woodland – of 2 furlongs by 1 furlong), Birstall (3 furlongs by 2) and Thurcaston (2 leagues by ½); the pattern of Leicester Forest, the hunting reserve of the twelfth century earls, becomes clearly designated – just twenty years after the Conquest. The later evidence relating to the manor of Thurcaston is highly relevant in this context. A charter of John of Gaunt, Duke of Lancaster, and dated 1384, acknowledges that:

> . . . *John Fawconer of Thurcaston . . . houldeth the mannor of Thurcaston of the said lord, as of the Honour of Leicester, . . . holden of the Forest Weynostre by petty serjeancy: that is to say, to keep falcons gemell ("twin" falcons) of the sayde Lord's . . . And it hath pleased the said council to declare that the said services have bin done to the said lorde . . . by Thomas Fawknor and his ancestors at all times after the conquest.*

The document goes on to name nine generations of the Falkener family of Thurcaston, beginning with William the Falconer at the time of William the Conqueror. The most fascinating question at this point is, however, who enfeoffed William as his falconer, Hugh of Grandmesnil or King William himself? Although Domesday Book clearly ascribes the whole manor of Thurcaston to Hugh, the entry for the lands of Geoffrey of La Guerche refers in three places to six manors given by William I 'in exchange for the village called Thurcaston'. As well as explaining the puzzle of the Thurcaston exchange, this evidence clearly shows that the Conqueror himself took an active part in the afforestation of this area forming the northern fringe of Leicester Forest. This was done either as a favour to his trusted vassal Hugh of Grandmesnil or, as seems more likely, Hugh was the instrument in the creation of a forest to the west and north of the town, later designated as a Royal Forest. Either way, we see in Domesday Book the creation of a chase called *Hereswode* already expanded to the north and west, and later known as Leicester Forest.

The same line of investigation can be applied equally fruitfully to the woodlands of that other great land owner and devastating hunter and fowler; Hugh of Avranches, Earl of Chester. The Earl's woodlands of his 'soke' estate centred upon Barrow-on-Soar (1 league by 4 furlongs at Barrow; 6 furlongs by 5 at Prestwold) along with those of Loughborough (7 furlongs by 3) and Dishley; and if, for the sake of this general hypothesis, these are seen in conjunction with the King's woodlands at Shepshed, they reveal an interesting correlation. As nuclei of afforestation in 1086 they exactly correspond to the chases and parks of that area which may be identified from later medieval evidence: Barrow, Beaumanor, Dishley, Loughborough, Shepshed. In this context, afforestation in the medieval sense, might well explain the designation of the earl of Chester's manor of Charley as *vasta* (waste). This is a much more convincing explanation than Stenton's theory of military devastation (p.31–32); waste through afforestation and the creation of chases is a regular feature of Domesday entries over a whole range of counties. Although the natives bemoaned the afforestation that indulged the Norman love of hunting, it at least served an ecological purpose by creating habitats for a whole range of wildlife. As the evidence of the *Anglo-Saxon Chronicle* and of Orderic Vitalis show, the Norman aristocracy from the Conqueror downwards much preferred boars to boors!

The evidence of Domesday Book, again used in conjunction with later sources, particularly the *Leicestershire Survey* 1130, throws considerable light upon the nature of the Honour of Leicester during its transition from castlery to earldom between 1068 and 1107 which involved the disinheritance of the Grandmesnil family and the creation of the Earldom of Leicester for the Beaumont counts of Meulan. The episode opens up a whole range of historical facets. It emphasises the territorial stability and integrity of the Honour despite the vicissitudes of its holders through forfeiture, lapse and regrant – so dramatically apparent in the history of the Honour between the Conquest and the establishment of the Duchy of Lancaster in the fourteenth century. The dubious process by which the earldom came into the possession of the Beamonts also throws light upon the nature and resources of an Earldom in Fee under the Norman kings.

The castlery granted to Hugh of Grandmesnil, a Norman lord from the Calvados region, shortly after 1068, was made up of a number of different elements, each essential for the proper exercise of the duties of the castellan. There were the estates that made up the Honour. With the exception of those centred upon Ashby-de-la-Zouch, the vast bulk of Hugh's manors were in the south of the county. An examination of his holdings in other Domesday shires, reveals a concentration of manors and lands in Northamptonshire and Warwickshire that, in conjunction with the south Leicestershire estates, creates a surprisingly compact patrimony, like that granted to Hugh of Grandmesnil's neighbour Henry of Ferrers forming the Honour of Tutbury. It also emphasises the point that both the Honours of Leicester and Tutbury were not only territorially compact but also *ultra comitatum*: in the case of Leicester, transcending the boundaries of three contiguous counties. But the Domesday Survey does not give a totally accurate picture of actual or *de facto* control, even for 1086. Aubrey of Couci, having failed in his task of holding the stormy Earldom of Northumberland, returned in disgrace to his Norman estates with his Leicestershire and other lands escheat (forfeited) to William: in the words of Domesday Book 'they are now in the King's hands'. By 1130, his manors of Wanlip, Saxelby and Shoby were part of the Honour.

The lands held by the widows of Anglo-Saxon husbands need also to be scrutinized. In the case of the Countess Judith – as no doubt in others – following

inset 3 Who was Hugh of Grandmesnil? A summary of his life . . . . Editor

Hugh inherited extensive estates in Calvados (central Normandy) in 1040 (see fig. 14) and, with his younger brother, refounded the abbey of Saint-Évroul in 1050, a house he continued to endow thereafter (e.g. from Leicestershire – p.39). Exiled from Normandy, c. 1059, by Duke William for involvement in contemporarily conventional baronial feuds, he was nonetheless recalled c. 1063 to help defend Normandy against Maine and Brittany and then to be made castellan of a Norman frontier castle, Neufmarché-en-Lions. In 1066, he was one of the assembly of Norman magnates summoned to counsel William on the advisability of fighting for the English Crown. Hugh obviously voted "yes", and he fought courageously at Hastings. On King William's brief return from England to Normandy in 1067, Hugh was give a key post, since by 1068 he was governing the people around and from Winchester, at which lay the treasury and regalia of the Anglo-Saxon kings. When in 1068 William required help against Eadwine and Morkar (inset 2), however, Hugh seems instead to have returned briefly to Normandy probably at the behest of his beautiful and – by implied chronicle report – his amorous wife Adeliza, who later appears holding land in Leicestershire, and who bore him ten children. Unlike others guilty of similar absences, Hugh did not forfeit all his English estates. On the major territorial division of the realm amongst the leading Normans in 1070–71, however, he was made castellan not of Winchester (was this a demotion?), but of Leicester, and either then or later sheriff of the county. Apart from his "honour" of Leicester, his Domesday estates were scattered over a number of other shires (p.26). In 1079–80, he acted as one of the leading conciliators following the estrangement in Normandy of William from his rebellious son Robert. Back in England, by 1088 Hugh is found supporting the rebellion of Bishop Odo of Bayeux at Rochester against William's son Rufus, now king of England, by harrying both his own county of Leicestershire (though presumably not his own estates) and neighbouring Northamptonshire. It was a miscalculation: the English themselves widely supported William Rufus; though once again Hugh appears to have been forgiven. Landed Normans like Hugh, however, had to live their lives incessantly on two fronts. By 1090 his duchy estates were being threatened by Robert of Bellême (and eventually by Robert Duke of Normandy) and had therefore to be defended, a stand being taken at the castle of Courcey. Now an old man and no longer fit to fight, he nevertheless negotiated with Duke Robert for the lifting of the siege of the castle which was eventually ended, ironically, with the arrival in Normandy for other reasons, of Duke Robert's brother William Rufus. Widowed, probably in 1091, it was symptomatic of the cross-channel life led by men like Hugh, that seven years later he is to be found back in England where, during his own last illness, he was received as a monk by the Prior of Saint-Évroul itself. He died on 22 February 1098. As in life, so in death . . . .: packed in salt and sewn tightly into an ox-hide shroud, his corpse was translated for burial back to the Abbey which he and his brother had re-established. Orderic, the chronicler of Évroul, who wrote the epitaph for Hugh's tomb, had good reason to eulogise him as an honourable lord, loyal to his friends, a valorous warrior – "terrible to the foe", and as a generous benefactor of Saint-Évroul. The views of the inhabitants of Leicestershire are not recorded.

feudal practice she was allocated a powerful 'protector' (inverted commas are very necessary here), Hugh of Grandmesnil, who appears as her tenant in a number of entries. Some tenants are more dangerous than others. By 1130, a portion of these estates have been incorporated into the Honour. If we add to all these the lands of Hugh's wife Adeliza, then the result is vitually intact: the Honour of Leicester as it was acquired by Edmund of Lancaster in the reign of Edward I (apart from the divided Winchester Fee). In the typical Norman manner, Hugh not only enfeoffed his wife, but very likely his son and heir Ivo with lands in Willoughby Waterless, Cadeby and the rich manors of Evington, Ingarsby and Ashby-de-la-Zouch. All the preparations for the creation of an aristocractic dynasty had been made. Unfortunately for the House of Grandmesnil, although the succession from Hugh to Ivo was accomplished; the new lord of the Fee was to encounter

a fatal political hazard.

In addition to the estates, the castellan of Leicester in 1086 controlled the castle, the *caput honoris* (the head place of the Honour) and the town: from which he exercised his jurisdiction; the *cum castro, sigillo et libertate gladii* of later documents relating to earldoms. Within the town, he possesses a cash income from the mint, most of the houses, two churches and 24 burgesses and other property held jointly with the king. If we see Hugh, in the town as in the county, as 'protector' of the holdings of Countess Judith, the *de facto* control of her urban assets strengthened his power and resources. According to Orderic Vitalis, Ivo (and probably his father Hugh) was governor of the town, held the office of sheriff and farmed the royal dues – almost all the assets required of a would-be earl.

In the event, Ivo lost everything through the political hazard of backing the wrong heir, Robert of

Normandy, twice after the Conqueror's death, and through the malice and ambition of his ancestral enemy, Robert of Beaumont, Count of Meulan. Beaumont made the right choice in backing both William Rufus and Henry I. By treachery and sharp practice with the support and connivance of King Henry, Robert obtained a mortgage of Ivo's lands and at the latter's death on crusade, took possession. But the Count of Meulan, favourite and adviser to Henry I wanted more than an Honour; however well endowed. He required to elevate the Fee of Leicester into an earldom. How he did so, and thus affected the vital transformation, is best described by his contemporary Orderic Vitalis:

The before mentioned count of Meulan craftily gained his position by means of Ivo's share, who was governor of the town and sheriff and king's farmer; and through the king's assistance and his own cunning he gained possession of the whole city (sic) and thereupon, being created an earl in England, he surpassed all the magnates of the realm and nearly all his own kinsfolk in wealth and power.

These three elements: control of town and castle; control of a large territorial Honour; and the connivance of a king, were the essential ingredients for the elevation to an earldom 'with castle, seal, and to hold freely by the sword' in Norman England. Yet the atmosphere of dynastic feuds, political and physiological hazards, when that was largely dominated by the great and capricious power of the Norman kings, was fraught with perils even for a powerful feudal lord of a conquering race.

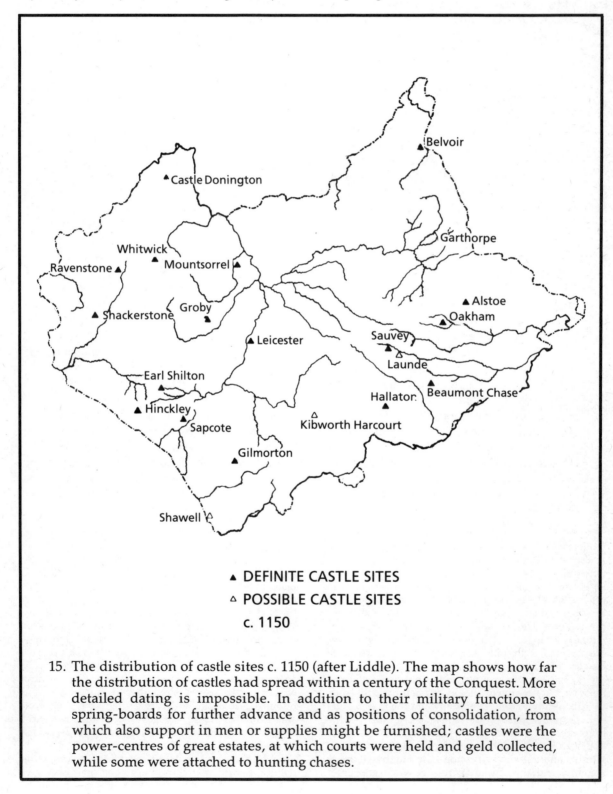

▲ DEFINITE CASTLE SITES

△ POSSIBLE CASTLE SITES

c. 1150

15. The distribution of castle sites c. 1150 (after Liddle). The map shows how far the distribution of castles had spread within a century of the Conquest. More detailed dating is impossible. In addition to their military functions as spring-boards for further advance and as positions of consolidation, from which also support in men or supplies might be furnished; castles were the power-centres of great estates, at which courts were held and geld collected, while some were attached to hunting chases.

4. THE SORTS AND CONDITIONS OF PEOPLE

Editor

Outside the towns in eleventh century Leicestershire and Rutland, as elsewhere, society was divided into three broad legal bands: the bond, the "free", and the lords. The varying social realities behind the statuses of the first two of these bands – those that concern us here – in large part depended on their standing *vis-à-vis* the third; for while all men had to be under some lord, the degree of subjection to the power of a lord varied. In addition, it is clear that the rank of man, as defined in law, did not necessarily equate with his economic standing or its lack.

The bond, or the unfree, comprised the slave-men and the slave-women (some of whom may have been the wives of the former). Such people might be bought and sold in exactly the same way as were cattle – before witnesses and with the payment of toll; they could be sent to live and to work where their owner willed; and by secular law, they might be flogged or even killed by their master without worldly – as opposed to eternal punishment. If murdered by others, their market price – usually the monetary equivalent of 4 oxen for a woman and 8 for a man – was payable to their owner to compensate him for the loss of his chattel. So low was the value set on the life of a slave by comparison with that of a "free" peasant, that the blood-money owed to the kindred of the latter as compensation (when death by blood-feud occurred) amounted to the same sum as that similarly payable to the relations of no fewer than 26 slaves. Slaves, it is clear, can have had no rights in a lord's court. To be freed from slavery, a man had to pay his owner 30 silver pence publicly as the "worth" of his skin or "hide". Small wonder then that, in early eleventh-century England, slaves sometimes ran away to secure their freedom even by fighting for the Vikings, and thus risked being stoned to death if they were caught.

Standing in relation to a lord also meant standing in relation to his land, the kernel of which in a manor was his demesne farm or, in the cases of large holdings, its offshoots – the berewicks (p.17). Both types of property were essentially commercial propositions and, if sufficient labour services were locally not available, had to be tilled by somebody. Even when demesne were obviously minute, therefore, a couple of slave-men might be kept on hand to steer the demesne plough and to lead its ox-team.

That anyway seems to have been the theory but, as so often in history, practice failed to match either legal or economic ideals. In our region there were neither enough slaves available to man all the demesne plough-teams, nor enough demesne teams to plough all the home farms. In the rather small demesne farms of the royal centres of Rothley and Great Bowden, indeed, as well as in the vast demesne estates of Queen Edith in Rutland, there were available no slaves at all. A place like Saltby with the excessive number of 6 demesne ploughs and no fewer than 16 slaves to work them, was quite exceptional. Had there been more ecclesiastical estates in the region, there might, perhaps, have been more slaves present in it; but the fact is that only about 6% of the recorded Domesday population of tenant-householders in Leicestershire were slaves, and only something in excess of 2% in Rutland. In the West Country, by contrast, some three times the Leicestershire proportion were in servitude. To ascribe this difference to the relative "freedom" of the Danelaw area as once used to be done, however, is hardly convincing. Other factors were also in play. The legal definitions of slavery described above, for example, blur the fact

that by the end of the Anglo-Saxon period, slaves may have become an expensive moral and financial luxury. By then, the church had long been advocating the emancipation of slaves for the eternal good of the slave-owners' souls (as well as for the immediate profit to the church, once a slave was freed and then had to pay church dues (p.42)). By then, too, slaves were becoming financially burdensome to their owners. Not only free lodging – whatever that may have comprised – but also "payments" by the lord of grain or of bread (720 loaves per year in addition to two meals a day, according to one authority) might be expected. In other words, a good deal of the crop harvested from demesne farms must have been immediately redirected away from the lord to the slaves who did the work.

Faced with such a problem when the need for incomes in cash was growing, the options open to a lord seem to have been two-fold: either he gave to his slaves a small area of land out of his demesne or out of his manorial waste, on which they might build their own cottages (and from which they would be expected to feed themselves) on condition that they continued to labour for him on other terms (he would normally emancipate them in such a case); or he looked elsewhere for the man-power with which to cultivate his lands. In practice it would appear that, by the eleventh century, and probably long before, many lords were already combining these two options. For some slaves at least, and despite their theoretical legal condition, this may thus have been an upwardly mobile society. To have been able to save "skin-money" alone for the purpose of self-emancipation, implies at least the possibility of acquiring a personal income from sources other than the lord, and an income that could never have been wholly at the disposition of such a lord.

The legal nature of bondage, however, is clear and it is against this measure that eleventh-century estimations of "freedom" have to be understood: to import modern preconceptions about liberty here would simply be anachronistic. In those days all freedoms were relative, and they were relative according to varying sets of criteria. The symbolic difference between servitude and freedom was expressed in the contrasting public rituals of enslavement and of emancipation. In the former case, the new slave was given an agricultural implement like a bill-hook; in the latter, the freed man was presented with a weapon, since from then on it would be his duty both to fight in battle when required and, as emblematic of his freedom, to brandish his weapon at the court of the wapentake (a recent interpretation of the name for the meeting-place of Gartree wapentake, indeed, suggests that this represented the tree or post where spears were flourished or hung up at such an assembly).

In practice, however, the difference between servitude and freedom was less clear-cut. Some men were in reality but half-free. The freed man set up as cottager by his lord with perhaps 5 acres of his land – in pre-conquest terms a *cotsetla* – continued to hold that land only at the will of the lord and in return for heavy labour weekly on the demesne farm. If he had time to spare he might eke out his living by hiring himself out elsewhere as a wage-labourer. Somewhat more fortunate, therefore, was the *gebur*, the boor, whose holding of perhaps 15 or 30 acres, some of them already sown, might be fitted out with a few livestock, and with tools and household utensils also provided by his lord whose property all these acquisitions remained. On the death of the *gebur*, land and the rest reverted to the lord. To judge from one Anglo-Saxon tract on *The Rights and Ranks of People*, the *gebur* will have driven himself to that grave early given the amount of ploughing and other work he had to do weekly on the demesne farm in addition to running his own farm, out of which he had also to find various payments in kind like hens, lambs, grain or honey with which to pay his rent and his church-taxes.

In Domesday book the *cotsetla* and the *gebur* seem to emerge in the terminology of the survey as the "bordar" and the "villein". The term "bordar" appears to take its meaning from the French word *borde* – edge – and may thus relate to the opening up of the waste land of a manor. When found in relatively sizable groups, indeed, bordars may sometimes represent batches of recently freed slaves who are being used for this purpose as perhaps in the cases of manors at Orton-on-the-Hill or Bottesford, where in each there were 13 bordars, or at Over Seal where there were 12, and Ashby Magna with 10. At Tolethorpe, Rutland, as at Bottesford, bordars outnumbered the rest of the population; in this instance by 15 to 12. Elsewhere they are more usually found in groups of less than 5. Over 1,600 such labouring small-holders were recorded throughout Leicestershire and Rutland.

The bordars, however, were heavily outnumbered by the standard farmers, the villeins, who totalled over 3,700 in the two areas. Within this rank there must have been wide extremes of wealth. Many villeins would have been prosperous enough to employ bordars on their farms; some seem even to have possessed slaves to judge for example from the Domesday entry for Burbage where it was said "20 villeins with 2 bordars and 2 slaves have 8 ploughs". It is apparent, nonetheless, that the villein wealthy enough to possess an entire team of 8 oxen was a rarity. The typical villein in Leicestershire appears to have owned only 2 or 3 plough-beasts, though by comparison with the bordars, many of whom clearly had no oxen at all, or at most 1 or 2, he was decidedly better-off. Even so, such rough calculations do emphasise that arable farming was above all a cooperative exercise: to make up a plough-team it was essential for a number of tenants to contribute a share of the oxen.

Whereas the villein took his status for the vill, the sokeman took his standing from the Soke or the sokeland which he occupied (p.17–18). Given the distance at which sokeland often lay from the parent manor, sokemen were more independent of the demesne farm than were the villeins. As we have seen, they also owned their own land as opposed to the "jurisdiction" over it. The labour-services which they performed for their lord thus seem to have been lighter, more occasional, and probably less demeaning than those owned by the villein. Evidence for Great Eaton on the Leicestershire-Rutland border not long after Domesday, suggests that in this case part of a sokeman's service may have been military. In other counties, the possession of horses by sokemen implies that they did riding-services for their lords. At Luffenham in Rutland, 12 sokemen and 16 bordars appear simply to have done "the king's work" as the reeve commanded.

Sokemen were farmers, nonetheless, and were not inevitably more prosperous than the villeins: if anything, they may have owned slightly fewer plough-beasts per head than did the villeins in Leicestershire, though since they probably did not do ploughing-services on their lords' demesne farms, this must be regarded as a misleading measure. The frequency with which sokemen are found side by side with bordars, as at Luffenham, moreover, may indicate that they often employed the latter. One king's sokeman, at least, was wealthy enough to hold a quarter of a substantial wood at Knossington; another sokeman at Sysonby was in possession of a whole plough-team.

On the ascending scale of freedom which underlies this discussion, it is apparent that sokemen were freer than villeins, though for our area the exact nature of that freedom is not evidenced in Domesday. Some scholars have argued that sokemen, who are found in profusion only in eastern England (there were over 2,000 in Leicestershire and Rutland alone, while in Framland wapentake they accounted for 50% of the recorded population), were the descendants of free Scandinavian settlers. Others have argued plausibly that their antecedents were more ancient still, and that the main burden of their renders and services was originally public – owed to the king – rather than manorial (p.18). It certainly seems to have been the case, that unlike the villeins, sokemen were responsible for their own geld-payments. To judge from later regional evidence, it is highly likely that another mark of their freedom lay in their ability to sell their land (though not the lord's jurisdiction over it) – a freedom that was not enjoyed by villeins. A second possibility is that, as in East Anglia where the Domesday evidence on this subject is far more detailed, even a sokeman who could not sell his land may nevertheless have been able to seek the protection (though not the jurisdiction) of one or even more lords other than the lord whose sokeland it was. Like those further up the social scale (p.23), he could "commend" himself to a lord of his choice for this purpose.

Whatever the case, it is possible that, as is evidenced in East Anglia, the numbers of sokemen had been reduced by the Norman Conquest. In an ideal world sokeland, unlike manorial land, should have continued to contain only sokemen (and perhaps bordars). Thus the parent *manor* at Somerby contained 5 villeins, a priest and 2 bordars; but the land belonging to it, at Little Dalby, was inhabited only by 16 sokemen who also had a priest. When therefore we read that the sokelands of one of the best preserved Sokes of Leicestershire, that of Melton Mowbray, contained "100 sokemen with 10 villeins and 13 bordars" in 1086, we may begin to suspect that the few villeins in question might well have called themselves "sokemen" 20 years earlier. Over the manorialising sokelands of Barrow-on-Soar, in Earl Hugh's holdings (p.18), 30 sokemen were actually outnumbered by 25 villeins and 13 bordars; in the similar holdings of his *milites*, there were 12 villeins, 2 bordars and but a single sokeman.

Given also the subsequent history of the "free" customary tenant, the villein, and the decline of his status into serfdom (so that he was even debarred from actions in the royal courts 200 years later), it may reasonably be observed that for many ordinary country-people, the Norman Conquest hardly resulted in a sudden access of human liberties.

PART III   LEICESTERSHIRE AND RUTLAND IN THE LATE ELEVENTH CENTURY

1. INTRODUCTION: THE "WEALTH OF THE REGION

Editor

When set against England as a whole in 1086 (and thus excluding the four northernmost counties which were not surveyed in Domesday Book), Leicestershire emerges in terms both of its population and wealth as a border area situated on the edge of the great divide between North and South. In the case of population, the county lay just within that zone of relatively high population density which was delimited to the north by an imaginary line running from the Severn estuary to the Humber. In the case of wealth, it lay outside the south-eastern zone of relatively high manorial valuation (if by such valuations we may infer annual financial yields to the lords concerned, whether these were actual or estimated) – the only measure of rural wealth that is available to us. Here, in broad terms, the line ran again from the Severn but this time to the Wash. On any of the measures presently available, Leicestershire's immediate neighbours – Warwickshire, Northamptonshire and most, if not all, of Lincolnshire – marked the southernmost limit of that half of England which reveals manorial values *below* the national average; the Rutland evidence being insufficient for inclusion. More than this, according to what may be the two most sensitive indicators of shire wealth (which are based respectively on averages of shillings for each recorded man and for each recorded plough-team, *per* county), Leicestershire itself emerges as not simply below the national average, but in both instances at a level representing no more than *half* the national average.

In 1086, Leicestershire may have ranked lower in terms of comparative regional wealth than at any period in the county's subsequent history. What then are we further to make of the astonishing fact that between 1070–71 (the likely date for the Norman land-settlement) and 1086, the Domesday valuations of Leicestershire manors appear to have doubled? On this evidence, if the people of Leicestershire were poor in 1086; they must have been existing on the margins of beggary 15 to 20 years earlier. But it was not only this that moved perhaps the greatest scholar of Domesday, F. W. Maitland, to describe the area as reflecting "prairie values". If the tax liability of Leicestershire is also taken into account, the number of carucates for which the county was answerable as a whole would have ensured a crippling fiscal burden on its inhabitants. In manor after manor, apparently, more tax would have been payable (when the geld was calculated at the usual rate of 2 shillings per carucate, let alone when, as in 1085, it was imposed at three times that rate) even than the valuation of each estate. To account for such low valuations and to confirm that Leicestershire's tax assessment was too high, two explanations have been offered.

On the one hand, it has been suggested that the low manorial valuations in the county, were the outcome of some previous period of military harrying. Excessively low T.R.E. valuations for some parts of the Welland valley (when these are measured against the increased later valuations said to be depicting recovery in 1086) are explained in terms of the devastation caused by Eadwine and Morkar in 1065 (inset 2). Low T.R.E. values broadly along the route of the Fosse Way towards Leicester are explained by the advance of King William from Warwick to Nottingham in 1068; and similar patterns, plus the Domesday evidence for what is there described as "waste", are held also to reflect an alternate approach towards Nottingham along the line of the county boundary between Leicestershire and Derbyshire – a possible avenue of approach for William's army had it advanced towards Nottingham from Warwick *via* Tamworth. In all such cases, allowance is made also for the destructive activities of raiding detachments and foraging parties in roughly adjacent areas.

Ingenious as such theories concerning Leicestershire's low valuation before Domesday may be, they are yet far from proven. First, the postulated depredations in Leicestershire of both 1065 and 1068 are not evidenced by any writer. In the former year Morkar's troops are scarcely likely to have ravaged a shire that lay within his own brother's earldom (fig. 13), whereas the spoliation of Northamptonshire – and therefore probably the Witchley Hundred part of Rutland – is evidenced not only in the Anglo-Saxon Chronicle but also in a geld roll for that county of c. 1075 which seems to indicate the extent of the destruction then wrought. Secondly, the evidence of chronicles for 1068 which together tell us the sequence of castles built by William at Warwick, Nottingham and at York on his outward journey; and *then* at Lincoln, Huntingdon and Cambridge on his return; conspicuously omits Leicester (unless Leicester is to be included in the phrase referring to castle-building "in so many other places in that part of the country", a passage which seems to refer to the southward journey *from* York, as opposed to the earlier advance towards it). Low T.R.E. valuations, in so far as they are consistently conspicuous at all along the line of the Fosse Way from Warwick to Leicester are thus not necessarily to be explained in this manner.

It is equally possible, but equally unprovable, that the Conqueror approached Nottingham along a line from Tamworth that was broadly coincident with the boundary between Leicestershire and Derbyshire. Certainly, Eadwine and Morkar are said to have submitted immediately following the fall of Warwick, so if the suggestion made earlier as to the possible possession of Leicester by Eadwine before this time is correct (p.19–20), it would not have been necessary for William to have taken the longer route *via* Leicester towards Nottingham. It could even be, then, that the pattern of wasted, or partially wasted manors, that tends to characterise both the two "sides" of the intermingled Leicestershire and Derbyshire border (and indeed also the neighbouring lands of these two shires and Nottinghamshire), may fossilize what have since been romantically described as "the footprints of the Conqueror".

Yet it has also to be said that 17 to 18 years is a very long time for land to remain wasted and hence agriculturally unproductive (the firing of stubble annually, after all, is now regarded as good farming practice), especially when the evidence shows that often only the component manors of vills – as opposed to whole vills – were so affected, and when a few such manors might still be worth some money, albeit of a slight order, in 1086. The fact is that Domesday uses the word "waste" to betoken many different things: in some instances it clearly refers to the transformation of an area into a hunting chase (p.26); in some, if depopulation is implied, it may mean that the tenants concerned have been deliberately and "peacefully re-planted" elsewhere for the purposes of rationalising the productivity of some wider estate; in yet others, it may simply indicate the relatively temporary dislocation in labour and materials (like the felling of trees in order to saw timber for palisading) that must have been created in woodland pasture areas especially by the construction of castles nearby. In any event, the central meaning of "waste" for the Domesday commissioners must surely have been to do with the inability, or the relative inability, of such places to answer for the geld or, if not, that it was not yet clear as to which centre or even in which county the tax owed from these areas was payable. It may not have been entirely accidental that such places as Linton, Donisthorpe or Ravenstone, which are described as waste or partially waste in Domesday, also lay along a band of territory within which the emergent shires of Derbyshire and Leicestershire (p.9) appear to have indecisively overlapped in wooded, or formerly wooded, country; and between which counties their allegiances were then and subsequently split (as broadly indicated only in fig. 5).

The other apparent indication of the wretchedness of life in Leicestershire stems from what seems to have been the county's heavy liability to tax (a matter of such serpentine complexity that some readers may now wish to skip immediately to the concluding paragraph of this chapter where a tentative judgement is reached). On this view – a long-standing interpretation that has recently been vigorously resuscitated – the county was ripe for a reduction of its assessment, and an exercise to this end was already in progress at the time of the Domesday Survey. If, it is argued, the carucate in some way once represented a form of assessment which was related to the plough (and thus also to the pasture needed to feed the oxen), then so too should it be accepted that when Domesday speaks of, for example, "land for" so many ploughs (that is, what historians usually abbreviate into the terms "ploughlands" or "teamlands"), we should understand thereby that some form of rate revision is to be inferred. In particular, it has been shown that often the number of carucates for which a vill or a manor was answerable to tax, appears to have stood in some blatantly artificial relationship to the number of ploughlands reported: sometimes in exact ratios of 3 carucates to 2 ploughlands; in other cases, in ratios of 2 carucates to 1 ploughland. From this it is argued that the ploughland should be regarded as the potential *new* unit of taxation, and that therefore in some parts of Leicestershire the tax-burden was in process of being reduced – and reduced appropriately – by a third or even a half. In privileged *Roteland*, by contrast, where significantly for this theory, the carucation is normally expressed as it *had* been T.R.E., an attempt may also have been made to change the assessment in an equally artificial way. In each of two small "hundreds" of 12 carucates (p.8), it is said in the Domesday introduction (fig. 1) "there *can* be 48 ploughs" (in fact there were 42, when these are added up for each vill). On this argument then, the logic would be that in *Roteland* the local tax assessment was being revised upwards.

Once again, unfortunately, this is a theory that still requires not only to be proved but also to be established in the light of the regularly differing terminologies used

in Domesday for the ploughlands of different fiefs in Leicestershire – a reflection, doubtless, of the manner in which the evidence was earlier collected. In such instances, it is still difficult to accommodate to this theory about plough-*lands*, such phraseologies to do specifically with *teams* rather than lands, as "x ploughs *were* there T.R.E.", or "there *were* y ploughs". That even aside, it is only fair to state that for one school of historians, the obviously artificial totals of ploughlands in *Roteland*, for example, ought to be seen not as new assessments but as positively *archaic* assessments that may reach back even to the days of the Scandinavian settlement. In other words, the carucation totals recorded there should be taken not as an indication of the area's rising liability to tax, but more properly, as defining a *reduction* in the area's fiscal burden!

What then should we make of this vexed and tangled web in the context of apparently marginal levels of wealth in the region? In the face of some flatly contradictory interpretations, let alone the inscrutability of the evidence itself, certainty is impossible. Nevertheless, some general points may be made. First, the argument favouring an earlier Scandinavian origin for the ploughland cannot easily be sustained. Numbers of ploughlands were clearly calculated at different times from actual numbers of ploughs. In some counties, including Northamptonshire – and hence the southern portion of Rutland – there is a close equivalence in Domesday between the contemporary totals for ploughs and ploughlands in large numbers of holdings. Commonsense alone rebels against the thought that the numbers of ploughs had remained more or less constant for up to 200 years. In such cases, therefore, (and the *Roteland* area may here be added), the inference must be that the ploughlands have been calculated fairly recently: if not in 1086, then at least not long before. In the case of Leicestershire by contrast, the general lack of an equivalence between teams and ploughlands and the variations in the formulas which declare the latter, would suggest that despite the fact that the totals of ploughs had been collected in 1086, the "official" conversion of ploughs into ploughlands had not been accomplished: in many cases references were still being made to the totals of actual ploughs that had been kept on the files since the time of King Eadward.

But, secondly, does this mean necessarily that the recalculation of ploughland totals should be taken to indicate that a process of fiscal re-assessment was in train but not yet completed? All that may be said at present is that if that was the case it seems curious that in some southern counties where the hide, not the carucate, was the unit of assessment, Domesday indicates that the numbers of hides themselves had been recalculated, for in those regions different figures are given for them both T.R.E. and T.R.W. If a reassessment based on ploughlands *was* intended, moreover, it was never carried out, despite what seem to have been the efforts made to screw up the yield of the geld in the following reign. *The Leicestershire Survey* of c. 1130, it will be recalled, shows the county still being taxed according to the same carucation levels as those recorded in Domesday.

If ploughlands may be accepted as fiscal units, however, an alternative solution to these problems might be very tentatively proposed. Geld was laid on defined units of land: if carucates were laid on each manor as a whole, may it not be that the ploughlands represented the formal *sub*divisions of each manor, the occupiers of which (whether or not they held actual ploughs) shared the total tax owed between them in due proportion? It is easy to see why, as population expanded or contracted, it would have been necessary to redefine such subdivisions. At any rate, we are not yet in a position to use this, or any other hypothesis concerning the ploughland, as proof that Leicestershire's overall tax burden was in need of downward revision.

More than this, there must also remain some considerable doubts as to whether Leicestershire's assessment was really as harsh as is sometimes implied. First, in terms of acres per tax-unit, the county did not fare all that differently from Berkshire, Buckinghamshire or Oxfordshire, none of which counties is usually characterised as poor. Secondly, and consequently, the case for the "poverty" of Leicestershire thus ultimately depends on the degree to which the low valuations of

Domesday are acceptable as they stand. If, as we have seen, they are not to be explained by theories of devastation, could it be that some elements included elsewhere in the valuations – like the sums paid when tenancies were first taken up, for example – were for some reason simply excluded in Leicestershire? It is impossible now to tell. Nevertheless, even if the levels of rural wealth in Leicestershire may have been below the national average at this time, we may well beg leave to doubt whether its supposed degree of "poverty" was quite as serious as it is sometimes stated to have been.

2. POPULATION, SETTLEMENT AND RURAL ECONOMY

Population . . . . Editor

There cannot be much doubt that by 1086, most of the settlements of modern Leicestershire and Rutland had already come into existence even though Domesday does not always name them. *The Leicestershire Survey* of *c.* 1130 adds 26 names (mainly in those northern parts of the county which it covers) to those listed in Domesday where, it seems likely, many such places were simply disguised under the composite entries for some larger estates. In Rutland, 19, possibly 20 dependencies of the three great royal manors in Martinsley wapentake are enumerated though not named in Domesday; yet broadly contemporary evidence indicates the existence in the manor of Ridlington, at least, of Ayston, Uppingham, Wardley and Belton: the remainder of such Rutland holdings being identifiable from sources that are not all that much later. Only Clipsham and Pickworth in the east do not appear to be accounted for in Domesday, but it seems likely that they too already existed – perhaps as detached portions of woodland which pertained, as in later times, to the manor of Oakham (and hence to the wapentake of Martinsley).

Despite what appears, throughout the region as a whole, to have been a relatively comprehensive coverage of settlements (including those later to be deserted), the reconstruction of population figures from the Domesday material is an especially hazardous undertaking. For a start, no evidence is supplied about the presence of resident lordly households, the numbers of followers in which may often have been substantial. Then too there is the insoluble problem of whom Domesday may have left out: in Staffordshire, for example, there seems to have been a class of rent-payers the like of which may have gone unrecorded in this region; in other instances, it is possible that a good deal of sub-letting to unreported tenants may have occured; while at some towns elsewhere there are indications of numerous cottage populations (at Warwick, they were probably market-gardeners) and even of "poor men", at neither of whose existence does the entry for Leicester even hint. Where male slaves are recorded, moreover, there is no way of deciding whether these were simply single young men or the mature heads of families. Finally, we can only guess that the average size of family may have been in the region of four to five members.

The most systematic modern attempt to convert Domesday statistics for the country as a whole into an estimate of "heads" (allowances being made for the missing counties of the North as well as, for example, the cities of London and Winchester) is that by Professor H. C. Darby. Depending on whether the average

household size was 4 or 5, he calculates that the possible total ranged from some 1,220,000 people to some 1,500,000, with most current historians probably favouring a figure at the upper end of this scale. In 1086, therefore, the entire population of England was not much different in size to that of the population of Leicestershire and Rutland today. It is possible indeed that in eleventh-century England, sheep outnumbered human beings in a ratio of three or four to one. Nor, it should be emphasised, was this population total vastly swelled by a massive Norman migration. A recent estimate suggests that under 2000 foreigners were granted land by the time of Domesday, and that the total migration across the channel cannot have amounted to more than 10,000 people.

The scale of settlement was thus inevitably smaller than today. The largest town in the east Midlands was Lincoln and that cannot have boasted much more than 6,000 inhabitants. Its nearest rival, interestingly enough, was probably Stamford with some 3,000, followed by Leicester and Nottingham with totals in the region of 2,000. However rough and ready such estimates are, we may safely say that many a modern village, like Great Glen in Leicestershire, can now boast a substantially larger population than the city of Leicester itself in Domesday.

In terms of contemporary size, however, Leicester towered over its nearest rivals with what looks like a minimal total of 387 householders (houses plus burgesses) (p.46). Below that level, some "larger" concentrations of rural population in the region may have been divided between one or more settlements or more than one manor: Bottesford (?78 + 22–?32 households), Empingham (65 + ?16) or Wigston Magna (?46 + 37) (queries denote problems about whether demesne residences ought to be included as they have been here). Interestingly, some of the more important "later" market centres emerge not only as one-manor vills, but also as places containing relatively strong concentrations of population. Oakham and Uppingham aside (since their populations are subsumed into composite entries), such places included Hinckley (?62 households) and Loughborough (?40); while the only definite market "town" in the area, Melton Mowbray, contained perhaps 37 households. At the other end of the rural scale, it is clear that a large number of rural settlements comprised no more than 20 households; some 80 places in Leicestershire contained 10 or less. As we shall see, the term "village" needs to be used with caution at this period.

Estimations of the total populations inhabiting each of the two districts under discussion vary only according to whether ancient or "modern" county boundaries are used to define the units of calculation. There is thus a reasonably close agreement that the rural population of Leicestershire hovered around the 6,400 "household" mark (i.e. including slaves), and that the inhabitants of Rutland amounted to some 1,480 households. By adding 400 households for Leicester we reach a figure of 9,280 households which, when multiplied by 5, yields a total of 46,400 souls in the region. Were we to add a further 3,000 people so as to include Stamford, we would not be far wrong in assuming an estimated population of 50,000 in this wider area as a whole. Given the fact that by such an operation we thus exclude much of the rural hinterland that looked into Stamford from both Lincolnshire and Northamptonshire, the proportion of people resident in settlements that might be described as "urban" now amounts to an exaggerated 10 per cent: the real figure must have been closer to five or six per cent. The world we have to investigate and understand, therefore, was quite opposite in its character to the modern experience of the town-dweller: in those days, perhaps 95% of the population depended on agriculture for a living. Take Oadby, for example; it is now one of the largest suburbs

of Leicester, but then it was an isolated rural vill containing perhaps 50 households.

That being so, it is essential to realise that the population of some 39,400 souls resident in the countryside throughout the region was not distributed equally across it. In highly generalised terms, the great divide was defined by the north-south axis of the River Soar. From there eastwards, and with but few exceptions, through to the Rutland boundary with Lincolnshire, rural settlements tended to be above the regional average in size and the density of population per square mile was reasonably high by local contemporary standards. To the west of the Soar, by contrast, settlements were normally more widely scattered and distinctly smaller. That not inconsiderable area, but excluding the Soar valley, contained no more than 1 in 5 of Leicestershire's total population. In Leicestershire, at least, it would not be until some five or six centuries had elapsed since the days of Domesday, that this disparity between the east and the west of the shire would be redressed in both economic and demographic terms. But that is another story. What matters here are the agrarian realities which lurk behind this division, and the ways in which the evidence of Domesday Book might help to explain them.

Settlement and the agrarian economy

The nature of the relationship betwen local environments and the societies which traditionally inhabited them is now broadly established. Because of the reluctance of many authors of school-text books to pay any attention to major advances in historical research of the kind that have now characterised as long a period as the last half century, however, it should be emphasised here both to those pupils and teachers alike who may read this publication that what is usually contained in such texts is not simply endearingly dotty: it actually falsifies past realities. Let us begin then by forgetting those neat diagrams of the three common-fields surrounding "the village" with its manor house and church, and concentrate on the far more interesting processes which helped to bring about a fascinatingly diversified pattern of responses from a traditional society that successfully survived without any of the benefits of modern technology.

Within the area of Leicestershire and Rutland alone, it is possible to identify three broad types of anciently contrasted environment: landscapes that then could have been paralleled again and again in other regions at the time of Domesday. Reduced to essentials these forms of environment may be crudely summarised as follows: the woodland districts (in which two important variations of the type may be identified); the former "wood-pasture" areas; and the landscapes of valley and vale. In distinguishing one from the other, however, it is vital to appreciate the differing stages of development that each had reached. We need to remember that Domesday furnishes us with no more than a still-picture, the processes that led up to which have to be reconstructed. Equally, the modern reader should never force in-built assumptions on so ancient a source. When Domesday names a settlement, for example, we simply cannot assume that this automatically implies the existence of an already developed village. Modern research is showing that, contrary to earlier opinion, the Anglo-Saxons did not bring with them, as it were, the idea and the form of the village with its adjacent common fields. Both these text-book features took a long time to develop and, for varying environmental, chronological and demographic reasons, at differing rates in different areas. In some regions, indeed, village formation (as the result either

of organic growth, when neighbouring farms or hamlets "grew" together as new housing was erected in the gaps between them, or of deliberately imposed planning) never even occurred; in other regions it occurred only during the continuing population expansion of the post-Domesday period. In weighing the contrasted characteristics of the three main types of landscape to be discovered in our region therefore, it will be necessary always to bear in mind the probable varying chronologies of settlement in each case, even though the space available does not allow of an extended discussion of these far from simple matters.

The first of the three types of landscape to be outlined is the woodland which characterised extensive tracts not only of west-Leicestershire but also of the upland areas of eastern Leicestershire, western Rutland and other parts of the latter district (fig. 16). The terminology of the more common Domesday measurement of woodland (x leagues by y leagues and z furlongs) makes it difficult to be certain about the densities of tree-coverage in these two separate areas (a Domesday league being usually taken to comprise 1½ miles), but there are indications that they should be contrasted. In west Leicestershire, for example the woodland entries are numerous and generous in their descriptions of extent. Since it is this very region which emerges as well-wooded in post-Conquest times – especially in the areas of the later "forest" of Leicester and the "waste" of Charnwood – there cannot be much doubt that a relatively dense zone of woodland, interrupted by forest glades and more open areas of sparse settlement stretched in all for some 25 miles from the Watling Street boundary, and then northwards to the west of the River Soar until it all but reached the Nottinghamshire border in the north, and the Derbyshire boundary on the north-west. It was no accident, therefore, that it was in this region that settlements lay less thickly on the ground than elsewhere, and that in terms of population density there appear to have been fewer than five households on average to the square mile. With but few possible exceptions, this could hardly be described as a classic area for the typical Midland village; it is much more likely to have been a landscape of scattered farmsteads and hamlets interspersed only occasionally by slightly larger settlements.

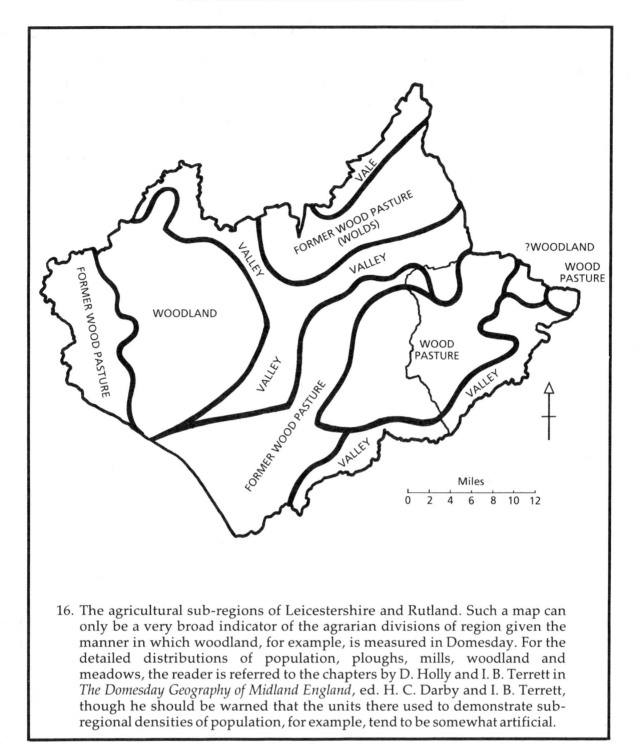

16. The agricultural sub-regions of Leicestershire and Rutland. Such a map can only be a very broad indicator of the agrarian divisions of region given the manner in which woodland, for example, is measured in Domesday. For the detailed distributions of population, ploughs, mills, woodland and meadows, the reader is referred to the chapters by D. Holly and I. B. Terrett in *The Domesday Geography of Midland England*, ed. H. C. Darby and I. B. Terrett, though he should be warned that the units there used to demonstrate sub-regional densities of population, for example, tend to be somewhat artificial.

In the upland areas of eastern Leicestershire and western Rutland, a contrast may be seen. In the case of the former, the woodland measurements given are smaller than those for western Leicestershire (sometimes they are in acres), and the impression left is that of relatively small woods dotted over a more open landscape – trees being interspersed with arable farming communities and their accompanying fields. Over the border, in the adjacent region of Rutland, moreover, woodland is normally described in two revealing ways: either it is woodland pasture or it is woodland with "pasture in places". In either case, we may infer that this is not thickly continuous woodland; even when large measurements are given, these are clearly aggregated totals, especially in the huge royal manors, and so they are no indication of consistently dense tree-cover. Nor could they be, given the densities of population in these areas: over nine households to the

square mile west of the Rutland boundary, and over eleven to the immediate east of it (though the Rutland densities decline towards the northern boundary). In both localities there were also between two and three times as many plough-teams to the square mile as in west Leicestershire (again, excepting northern Rutland); arable farming had therefore advanced further. For these and other reasons, both archaeological and topographical, in fact, there is good cause to suspect that by 1086 this district had been systematically exploited for longer, and therefore settled earlier, than was the case in west Leicestershire.

Such woodland economies were vital to contemporaries. Of the most obvious uses of wood, for fuel and building materials, we hear nothing from Domesday, which is equally silent on the matter of industrial processes requiring large quantities of firing in pottery kilns or for metal-working as may have been the case within the precincts of Hallaton castle. The nearest hint is the occasional mention of what could have been coppice wood – at Bisbrooke (Rutland) or at Measham on the Leicestershire-Derbyshire border. Woodland grass, however, was clearly essential for grazing, being cropped, we may reasonably guess, by both free-ranging cattle and sheep which would periodically be rounded-up. It is noticeable that in very general terms, the greater the area of woodland, the less frequent and usually the smaller are the meadow-lands which are nevertheless found quite extensively where woodland pasture was not available. The nearest we can get to the use of woodland by pigs in the region is with reference to woodland for 100 swine at Ashby-de-la-Zouch, a figure which is probably best treated as an estimate of how many pigs might theoretically be fattened off the beach mast and acorns available each autumn. We know from elsewhere, however, that such herds of small pigs might run into hundreds, and that this was one of the more widespread practices of woodland agriculture in the eleventh century. The frequent presence of root-grubbing swine in woodland areas, indeed, must have been a major factor in stopping woodland regeneration.

A final aspect of woodland economies tends sometimes to be forgotten. At this period, of course, such areas were teeming with wild-life (though it is likely that both rabbits and fallow-deer were a Norman introduction) which consequently was an important source of both food and sport. The Crown expected the annual render of a hawk from the City of Leicester, while at both royal and aristocratic levels there are a few signs, even before the Conquest, that some areas may have been regarded as privileged for the purposes of hunting. It is possible for example that Queen Eadgyth's lands in Rutland as a whole were of this kind, since they are later found to be almost co-terminous with the Forest of Leighfield – a subdivision of the later royal forest of Leicestershire and Rutland. It was the Normans, nevertheless, who imposed tight restrictions on hunting through their development of the Forest Law (p.24–26) – the word "forest" here being used as descriptive of an area, whether wooded or open, in which rights of hunting were reserved to the Crown – and of rights of private chase.

Such factors indeed clearly affected the distribution of motte-and-bailey castles in the region during the late eleventh and early twelfth centuries (fig. 15). Like the earlier royal hall at Oakham, perhaps, the majority of Norman castles were situated in or beside areas known from Domesday to have been wooded: Alstoe, Hallaton or Castle Donington, for example. Leicester "forest" was surrounded by castles – at Leicester itself, Groby, Earl Shilton and probably Sapcote (in all of which vills, land was held by Hugh of Grandmesnil in 1086); Beaumont Chase on the edge of Rutland was probably appendant to the motte-and-bailey castle on Castle Hill to the west of Uppingham; while Sauvey castle was to become a major centre for the later royal forest of Leicestershire and Rutland. Of the earlier castles, only Belvoir may have been an exception, though there woodland may have gone unrecorded in 1086: 100 acres of spinney are reported at Redmile 200 years later. In one sense, therefore, a new kind of later settlement was thus superimposed on woodland landscapes with its own type of "farming". Whoever else went short during the winter, castle garrisons would have been sure of a supply of venison and other game (let alone fuel as well as timber for the palisading (p.32)). In such instances, hunting might be seen as a distinctive part of the demesne economy.

If Domesday hints at different degrees of clearance in the two major woodland areas of the region, a further type of landscape, perhaps best described as "former wood-pasture", may be shown to have been cleared centuries before. While the whole of the upland region of north-east Leicestershire is a blank so far as woodland is concerned in 1086, suggestive elucidatory work by Professor Alan Everitt has shown that at some earlier stage in the Anglo-Saxon period it was probably covered with trees. The topographical history of the area is symbolised in a single place-name, Waltham-on-the-Wolds. In Old English, "Waltham" means the "homestead" (ham – one of the oldest English place-name elements to denote habitation) in the wald or forest; wold, a linguistically related term, refers to an area, usually of upland, that had since been cleared of its trees. When, therefore, we recall the names of the settlements that stretch from Prestwold, Wymeswold and Burton-on-the-Wolds in the west to Waltham in the east, as well as the wold country which reaches north of Willoughby-on-the-Wolds on the Nottinghamshire boundary, we may reasonably infer that this zone of north-east Leicestershire had once been wooded (in Domesday, part of Prestwold still was). A similar area lay just over the south-western county boundary with Warwickshire in the region of Wolvey Wolds, and it may not be without significance that the only contemporary "evidence" we have for woodland clearance in Leicestershire comes from the nearby parish of Claybrooke. There in 962, a small surviving block of woodland covered some two-thirds of the township of Claybrooke Parva, to judge from the bounds detailed in the charter of that year. In 1086, however, no woodland at all is recorded for the entire parish (fig. 9). Claybrooke may perhaps be taken as representing a broad arc of territory north of the Welland valley and stretching from the Fosse Way on the west towards the still wooded regions of east Leicestershire. In this area, to judge from many detailed topographical clues (Cotesbach by Lutterworth had a field called "Smallwold"), woodland had been cleared long before Domesday, but left behind it areas of residual scrubland, usually near parish boundaries, and often now known in characteristically local terms as Bosworth Gorse, Whetstone Gorse, Glen Gorse, Norton Gorse and so on. A similar countryside – some of it heathland – may reasonably be postulated in the extreme west of the county.

In such a landscape, Domesday reveals a relatively close pattern of middle-sized to small settlements (often within relatively small township areas), and average population densities of around nine householders per square mile, except in the west of the county where the figure drops to about four (readers should be warned that on some distribution maps the northern wolds area has been inaccurately plotted and the resulting figures may be misleading). Significantly there were over twice as many plough-teams per square mile as in the western woodlands. Even so, the area was markedly less well-endowed in this respect than the wood-pasture areas to the east. For an area of mixed farming, indeed, its main disadvantage must have been lack of pasture. The benefits of woodland grass had long since disappeared, and while this type of countryside could boast more meadow and more extensive meadows than were to be found in the wood-pasture regions, they were never very large, so other solutions to the problem of supplying grazing would have had to be sought. It was probably factors such as these, coupled with population pressure eventually, that led to the adoption in these areas of the classic Midland common-field system, with pasture in successive years made available in an annually-rotating fallow field. Certainly grain production in such districts was already developed by the time of Domesday to judge from the more intensive distribution of mills therein, as opposed to the relative paucity of mills in the woodland areas of both Leicestershire and Rutland.

The third and last characteristic landscape of our region as a whole was that of the valleys and vales. Theoretically, the rivers themselves should have provided a further natural resource: fisheries were listed, for example, along the Nene, the Trent and the Warwickshire Avon, but not along the Welland or the Soar: probably yet another indication of the unsatisfactory nature of much of Domesday's coverage of the region. The rich alluvial lands and, in some cases, their attendant gravel terraces, however, had long attracted settlement both in the Anglo-Saxon and the Danish periods. It is not in the least surprising, therefore, to find the highest densities of population in such areas and especially along the lines of the Wreake (the importance of which in this connection is disguised on some published maps); along the north side of the Welland, where the density ranged between nine and twelve householders per square mile; in the Vale of Belvoir, where it exceeded ten; and above all in the central valley of the Soar where it reached a density of nearly fifteen householders to the square mile. If developed villages, with their attendant common fields, were already in existence by this period, it would thus be in the anciently settled valley landscapes that we would most expect to find them. Unlike all the other sub-regions, moreover, the royal wood-pasture area of Rutland only excepted, the landscapes of valley and vale alone could boast roughly three to four plough-teams per square mile, teams that obviously could be fed off the meadows that were generally larger and more frequent in such locations than elsewhere. At Stapleford on the upper reaches of the Wreake, meadow amounting to 100 Domesday acres (whatever these may have comprised) is noted, while the combined total for nearby Wymondham and Edmondthorpe reached 130 acres. (By Domesday standards in some other counties, meadows of this size would have made some dairy-farming possible). Clearly, however, it was in the valley and vale landscapes that corn-growing was most productive: in such locations mills might be found not only in ones, but also in twos, threes or even more. Most remarkably of all, the river Devon in the north-east tip of Leicestershire, which pours down into the eastern end of the Vale of Belvoir, may have powered seven mills at Knipton and a further seven at Bottesford; while at Empingham on the river Gwash, no fewer than twelve mills are enumerated. Mills might be speculative investments by manorial lords who may have required tenants from further afield to bring their grain to be ground for a fee, yet concentrations of these magnitudes suggest areas nearby of substantial corn-production: in the cases specified at least, areas that looked also to urban markets as their outlets at Grantham and Stamford.

In the broadest possible outline, this is about as far as it is safe to go on the evidence available. The existence of contrasting agrarian economies within the several sub-regions discussed, however, should not be taken to indicate that each one would have been instantly distinguishable from its nearest neighbour within the space of a short distance. Such landscapes invariably fused gradually and imperceptibly into one another. All that could be done in the space available here was to point up the salient differences, and much room remains for the detailed work into this subject that is still desirable.

The problem of rural "marketing"

The world under discussion did not belong to some mythical golden age of peasant subsistence and parochial isolation. On the one hand, each individual manor normally belonged to some wider estate unit often with a centre many miles away. Such wider estates, it is clear, were run on hard-headed business lines by their new lords, the component manors of such units being distributed over more than one type of farming countryside. On the other hand, it should be stressed that it is becoming increasingly probable that the economy in general was rather more "sophisticated" than was once thought. Urban life was expanding and very considerable quantities of coin were in circulation. While many manorial tenants doubtless still answered for their lands in labour-services or renders in kind, many must also have paid their rents or their renders to Soke-centres in cash. The value of the *soc* of 2 carucates at Blaston, for example, was 11s ½d, a total that is hardly likely to be disguising a valuation of so many hens or whatever. Some bordars may have been paid cash wages, while the high scale of monetary fines liable for a whole range of offences, let alone the money paid in geld, also suggest that this was at least in part a cash economy.

The eleventh century peasant thus required coin for many purposes (at Birstall, the valuations are couched in ounces of gold), and not least with which to purchase for himself such commodities like iron, salt or pottery, quite apart from cattle, the proof of purchase of which figures prominently in the later Anglo-Saxon laws. How then was he to raise this cash? The answer must be, in the local market. Unfortunately, on this as on much else, Domesday remains obstinately silent. It fails even to mention a market at Leicester (p.47) – the only place in Leicestershire and Rutland at which coins were actually minted – although the earliest market site is situated in such a way as even to suggest a continuous history for it since days of the Roman forum. The only market mentioned by Domesday in either territory, in fact, was that at Melton Mowbray which appears to have transacted a sufficient volume of business to enable it to profit its lord to the not inconsiderable sum of 20 shillings annually. That this sum represents no more than a percentage of the total cash transactions involved in this market, we have no need to doubt.

That landholders other than Leofric, son of Leofwine, and his successor at Melton, Geoffrey of la Guerche must also have held this privilege is indisputable. Once again, the short-hand nature of the Leicestershire and Rutland entries may be concealing the possession of a quite widely held right. In the Nottinghamshire Domesday for example, it is clear that those holding the highly prized privilege of *sac* and *soc* (p.22–23), also held the additional rights of *toll* and *team* in all or many of their estates. These were the rights to take both a toll on all sales transacted and, where the theft of cattle in particular was alleged, the profits that came from the procedures for dealing with such disputes: privileges therefore which may indicate the existence of rural markets. The Nottinghamshire list includes the names of a number of Leicestershire landholders: pre-Conquest holders like the Countesses Godgifu and Aelfgifu (fig. 12) and the thegn Toki (p.13); and later Norman holders like Earl Hugh (p.24, 26) and Henry of Ferrers (p.26). Are we then to assume that men or women of this rank lacked similar rights in Leicestershire? It has already been pointed out that if the attachment of town houses in Leicester to rural manors had something to do with marketing, then it is curious indeed that not all tenants-in-chief seem to have had that convenience, however far away their estates may have lain.

Elsewhere, and indeed as at Melton (p.12), market centres often appear to have coincided with the locations of minster churches – a suggestion which seems to correlate with known Anglo-Saxon efforts to suppress Sunday trading (is there anything new under the sun?). Unfortunately in our region the recording of minsters in Domesday is practically non-existent, but a fair guess can be made as to their locations in some instances from later evidence. On such a slight basis, it may at least be tentatively proposed that known *later* medieval market centres such as Hallaton (Toki) and Castle Donington (Countess Aelfgifu) may have boasted markets earlier, as may have Hinckley (Earl Aubrey, but whose T.R.E. *antecessor* is not recorded)

with its uncharacteristically high population for the sub-region in which it was situated (p.34–35); while it would have been odd indeed had the King himself not had such rights, as well as minsters, at the centres of his two Sokes of Rothley and Bowden (out of which Market Harborough later emerged on a better site); and the last Anglo-Saxon Queen not had a similar privilege at Oakham where a prescriptive market is known to have existed from later evidence. If, as with so much else in Domesday, we may only guess; at least we should not make the mistake of believing that its silence on a matter is conclusive proof that the features of contemporary society concerned did not then exist.

---

3. CHURCHES AND CHURCHGOING IN 1086

Introduction . . . . David Parsons

In the days of Eadward the King . . .
This is a formula which is applied throughout Domesday Book to refer to conditions obtaining before the Norman Conquest. The commissioners used the value of property in the Confessor's reign as a point of comparison for their own findings. Similarly, when attempting to interpret the evidence for churches at Domesday, we need to look back at the Anglo-Saxon period to find their historical context.

Unless we think the Domesday evidence so defective as to be utterly meaningless, the first obvious conclusion to draw from it is that the system we are familiar with of 'one village – one church' had not yet developed. Approximately 50 churches are implied for Leicestershire and 14 or 15 for Rutland. These figures compare unfavourably both with the modern tally of about 400 churches and chapels (inflated though it is by the multiplicity of parishes in Leicester and the other towns) and with the total number of places listed in the Domesday survey. The ratio of "villages" to churches was about 6:1.

The reason for this lies in the Anglo-Saxon system of church organisation. The laws of King Aethelred ('the Unready') and King Knut ('Canute') earlier in the 11th century define the following categories of churches:

(a) chief minsters, usually cathedrals, serving a diocese or similar large area;

(b) lesser minsters, serving small areas within a diocese, though these areas were much more extensive than the average modern rural parish;

(c) minor churches with a graveyard;

(d) field churches.

The two classes of minster, often founded on royal land and at the centre of large estate complexes, were the 'official' churches, intended to minister to the needs of the population at large. The small churches, whether or not they had a graveyard, were essentially private chapels, erected and paid for by less important landowners for their own convenience or for the good of their souls. The owners of these private chapels still had to pay their dues to the local minster or mother

church, which continued officially to provide the main spiritual services for them and the people living on their estates. Some of these services attracted a fee. For example, there was 'soul scot', a kind of death duty payable at a funeral. Such fees provided the minsters with part of their income, and they were unlikely to relinquish their rights to a small private chapel if they could avoid it. But the need to be buried at the minster must have been a great inconvenience to everyone except those fortunate people who lived in the village where the mother church was. The others would have to bring their dead from outlying settlements, sometimes over considerable distances, and then pay for the privilege of burial at the minster. So landowners tended to negotiate the transfer of burial rights to their own local churches, and where they were successful a 'field church' would become a 'minor church with graveyard', and take a major step in the direction of becoming a parish church as we understand it.

Other payments apart from soul scot were due to the mother church, including tithe, but from as early as the 10th century it was permissible in certain circumstances for the owner to pay one third of the amount to his private chapel to defray running costs. One of the conditions was that the church should have a churchyard. Despite the gradual development of parish churches these primitive arrangements persisted in many places. The case of Staunton Harold, where a private chapel was established (or perhaps merely confirmed) in the 12th century is illuminating. The chaplain there was permitted to perform all ecclesiastical functions except burial; for that the inhabitants had to go to the mother church at Breedon, where in addition all the tithes had to be paid. Incidentally, the Staunton people were also obliged to go to mass at Breedon on St Hardulf's Day, the patronal festival. On the other side of the county Great Easton was still officially a chapelry of Bringhurst in the 14th century, and acquired its graveyard and attendant burial rights in 1349 only as a temporary measure because of the number of deaths caused by the plague.

Churches after the Conquest

The evidence of the Domesday survey of Leicestershire and Rutland seems to indicate an intermediate stage between the old minster system and a fully developed parochial one. But what Domesday Book

tells us is unfortunately not entirely straightforward. In Leicestershire proper hardly any churches are referred to. Of the six specifically mentioned, all were in the borough of Leicester; four belonged to Hugh of Grandmesnil, a great Leicestershire landowner, and two to the Bishop of Lincoln. Over the rest of the county the references are to priests in their capacity as members of the rural population. (In three cases priests are recorded as landowners, and they are probably not relevant to the present discussion.) It is a reasonable – though far from proven – assumption that each of these priests implies the existence of a local church. In a few cases it is possible to confirm this assumption. The history of Orderic, written between 1123 and 1141, records a series of grants made by Hugh of Grandmesnil and members of his family and confirmed by royal charter in 1081. In four cases churches are specifically mentioned at places where a priest is noted in Domesday (Carlton Curlieu, Noseley, Glenfield, Peatling). At a further two places (Earl Shilton, Langton) a grant of tithe implies the independence of a local church from the original minster and thus confirms the interpretation of priests mentioned there at Domesday. Churches are also referrred to at Belgrave and Thurcaston and grants of tithe at Stoughton and Thurmaston. At none of these places is a priest recorded at Domesday and this suggests that there may have been far more churches in 1086 then the survey implies. There are certainly several places in Leicestershire at which one would expect to find a church but where Domesday says nothing about a priest. Great Bowden was the centre of a large royal estate and should have had a minster church; Earl Hugh held Barrow-on-Soar from the king and its attached sokelands were even more extensive than Bowden's, but again no church was recorded.

On the other hand, Melton Mowbray seems to preserve some aspects of former minster status. Again it was the centre of a large Soke, whose outlying villages (several of which still belong to Melton for church purposes) are listed in Domesday Book. The survey lists not one but two priests, presumably the remnant of the staff of clergy appropriate to an Anglo-Saxon collegiate church. Two clergymen (a priest and clerk) are also mentioned at Wigston Magna, and a priest with a deacon at Market Bosworth. It is not clear whether minsters are implied.

In Rutland, however, the persistence of the old form of organisation comes through particularly clearly. Two royal estate centres, Hambleton and Ridlington, are credited with seven dependencies each, but these places are not named. The Hambleton estate had three priests and three churches, and the Ridlington estate two priests and three churches. The locations of the churches are not given and it is apparent that the estates were still considered as undivided units for ecclesiastical as well as administrative purposes. One church in each case was presumably at the estate centre, perhaps with the priests as a central staff of clergy. Later evidence suggests that the two churches dependent on Ridlington were probably at Uppingham and Wardley. Oakham similarly was the centre of a royal estate, with five unspecified dependencies, but there was only one church and one priest. Later in the Middle Ages Oakham had a number of dependent chapelries, some of which eventually became parishes in their own right (e.g. Langham). All this evidence comes from Martinsley wapentake, the core of what was to become Rutland, and was recorded by the Nottinghamshire enumerators. They also listed a church and priest at

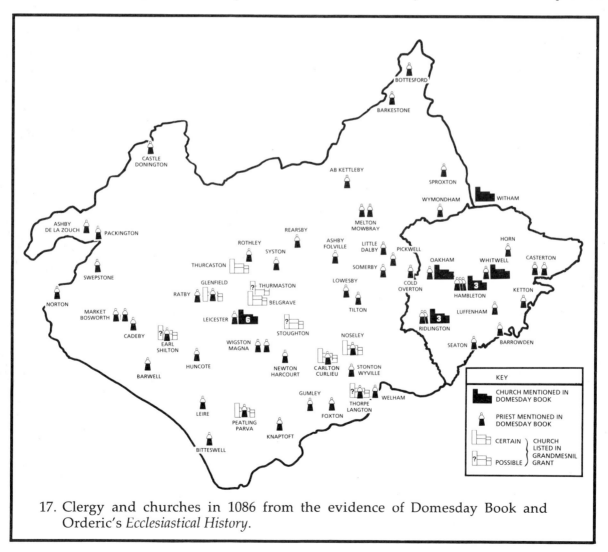

17. Clergy and churches in 1086 from the evidence of Domesday Book and Orderic's *Ecclesiastical History*.

Whitwell in the southern hundred of Alstoe wapentake. The remaining information for Rutland comes from Witchley hundred, consisting of the eastern part of the county and the strip adjoining the Welland. At the time this area belonged to Northamptonshire and was on the same enumerator's circuit as Leicestershire. Not surprisingly, only priests are listed in this hundred. Most of them are on royal land. In only one case, Barrowden, is there an extensive estate which might lead us to expect a minster. The one priest attached to the estate must have been overworked, though at Luffenham and Seaton, parts of which belonged to Barrowden, there were priests living on property not belonging to Barrowden. There were two priests at Casterton, but on separate estates, and they do not imply the former presence of a minster.

All this information is summarised on the map (fig. 17), which clearly shows how patchy the provision of churches was if the Domesday evidence is taken at face value. In theory the gaps might be filled by plotting those churches where early medieval fabric has survived. Unless there was an incredible spate of church building in the twenty years following the Norman Conquest, most of the churches at Domesday must have been Anglo-Saxon buildings. Unfortunately there is a dearth of pre-Conquest churches in Leicestershire and Rutland. The best example is St Nicholas, Leicester (fig. 18) where the side walls of the nave contain late

18. St Nicholas, Leicester:

Saxon windows and where the base of the tower may incorporate the Anglo-Saxon chancel; this was probably an early monastery and it may have served as the cathedral of the short-lived bishopic of Leicester in the 8th century. St Nicholas' was almost certainly one of the six Leicester churches mentioned in Domesday. Equally important are the surviving Anglo-Saxon friezes at Breedon-on-the-Hill, where there is in any case documentary evidence for a monastery by the end of the 7th century. Nearby Diseworth seems to be Saxo-Norman in date. Apart from this there is only minor evidence: a window at Birstall, and another at Foston, which may be early Norman rather than Saxon, though it could still qualify as fabric of the Domesday period (fig. 19). In Rutland there is only Market Overton, where the tower arch built in a pre-Conquest technique is complemented by pieces of Anglo-Saxon carved stonework.

Known Anglo-Saxon churches, then, do not add a great deal to the Domesday information, but sculptural remains are rather thicker on the ground. Grave slabs such as those at Hallaton or Harston imply an Anglo-Saxon burial ground and therefore presumably a church, while interlace or figural panels, for example at Great Glen or Foxton, suggest a stone building, which is more likely to have been ecclesiastical than secular. Fig. 20 shows where such remains are to be found. The sites of surviving sculpture and of early fabric taken together do fill some of the gaps in the Domesday map, especially in the Vale of Belvoir, but there is still a surprising lack of evidence in the centre of north Leicestershire.

19. St Bartholomew, Foston: Norman north arcade cutting earlier window, possibly of pre-Conquest date.

20. Distribution of pre-Conquest carved stonework in Leicestershire and Rutland (after Clough *et al.*, *Anglo-Saxon and Viking Leicestershire*, 1975, facing p. 92, with additions).

Getting there

Even taking the patently defective Domesday evidence on its own, the distribution of churches was less sparse than the 6:1 ratio might imply. By drawing circles round the places in fig. 17 it can be shown that hardly any inhabited part of Leicestershire was more than 5 miles as the crow flies from the nearest church, and (except in central north Leicestershire) few were more than 2½ miles away. The idea that people lived a very long way from a church will not stand scrutiny, though it must be admitted that we do not know whether they were free to attend any church of their own choosing if there were no chapel on the estate to which they belonged. If the only alternative was to go to the mother church, then in some cases worshippers would have a fairly long trek. Before there was a church at Eastwell, the villagers would have had to go 6 miles to the mother church in Melton, but if they were at liberty to attend the church at Barkestone the journey would have been reduced to 4 miles. If the Anglo-Saxon carved stone at Stathern is taken to indicate a church there, then the inhabitants of Eastwell will have had less than 2 miles to walk. Of course these are minimum distances, and even the average 2½ miles by winding road, by track or across the fields would have taken a long time, especially in bad weather. Churchgoing, particularly for the very young, the very old, and the infirm, must have been infrequent and limited to the major festivals and special occasions. Even the number of these would have been restricted. For instance, the birth of a baby would not necessarily lead to attendance at church, since the administration of baptism was legally confined to Easter and Whitsun; the parents would probably attend on these occasions in any case. Only in those places where there was actually a church, and in Leicester, where there were six churches, plus probably St Margaret's outside the walls, would the pattern of churchgoing have been markedly different.

For those who did not live in any out of the sixty or so privileged places, contact with the church must have been slight. But it is possible that if people could not get to a church, the church came to them. In the missionary phase of English Christianity in the 7th century we hear of bishops (who originally had 'paro-chial' responsibilities) touring their vast dioceses, teaching and administering the sacraments. The early subdivisions of the dioceses were also fairly extensive, and it is assumed that these peripatetic functions were taken over by the minster clergy. The likelihood that this system continued in places where there were few local churches is borne out by the number of portable altars that have survived from the early Middle Ages up to the 12th century. Such altars would be required for *ad hoc* masses celebrated by itinerant priests in unconsecrated buildings. By the 13th century most places had a church and (in theory at least) a resident clergyman, and the need for portable altars declined. They were still used in the later Middles Ages, but only in special circumstances and if authorised by the bishop.

Given the number of clergy in Domesday Leices-tershire, however, people living in remoter parts are not likely to have received communion in this way very often, even if the system did continue to operate in the late 11th century. The extent to which the Church impinged on their lives must have been rather limited. Indeed, they were probably aware of the Church less for its spiritual benefits than for its propensity for relieving them of a variety of taxes in cash or kind. Tithe (a tenth of the produce of the land) and soul scot have already been mentioned; there were also church scot (a grain render at Martinmas), plough alms (one penny per annum for each plough), light dues (a halfpennyworth of wax at three major festivals annu-ally) and Rome scot ('Peter's Pence': a contribution to the maintenance of the English School in Rome). Not all of these necessarily fell upon the individual, but it must have been clear to all that the Church was a great collector of revenues.

In Church

Those who did manage to get to church would have found themselves in a very different environment from that of the modern worshipper. In the first place, the average local church was a small building capable of holding only two or three dozen people. There were no side aisles, only a box-like nave with a small chancel to the east. Some churches had a tower, usually at the west end, and in a few cases (e.g. Earl's Barton in Northamptonshire) the body of the church consisted solely of the ground floor of the tower. There were no seats for the public, who would have had to stand throughout the services, though there may have been benches against the wall for the infirm, as there were later in the Middle Ages. The tradition that we have inherited from the 19th century of a remote altar at the far end of a chancel heavily screened-off from the nave had not yet developed. The conduct of a church service in the 11th century would have been much more like the revised liturgy that has developed in the last two decades. The altar was at the east end of the nave or just inside the chancel. In the case of a nave altar, the priest probably stood under the chancel arch and celebrated the mass facing the people. If the altar was just east of the chancel arch, the priest may still have celebrated westward from a position in the middle of the chancel. However, the period of Domesday seems to have been one of liturgical change and in some churches the priest may have continued to stand under the chancel arch, but now facing east to celebrate, with his back to the congregation. In either case, though, given the size of many churches and the probable position of the main altar, the people must have been more closely involved in the performance of the mass than they were to be later in the medieval period. In church the priest was among the people just as in the countryside he appears from the Domesday Book entries to have been an integral part of the farming community, sharing the communal ploughs with the ordinary villagers. Nine hundred years on, we find the supposedly 'modern' concepts of westward celebration and worker priests already foreshadowed at Domesday.

4. LEICESTER AT DOMESDAY

Allen Chinnery

The entry about Leicester itself in Domesday Book gives us the first statistical information we have about the town. However, it does present certain difficulties and much can only be understood if the pre-existing town is, to some degree, kept in mind. Similarly, although Domesday tells us a little about the way the town's life and topography were arranged, it is necessary to come a little forward in time and use records of a slightly later date to infer what was happening in 1086.

In the Domesday Book Leicester is treated in an entirely different way from the rest of the shire. Either when the West Saxons reconquered the Danish area of the Midlands in the tenth century or at some later period in the eleventh century, shires were created so as to centre on large existing towns with the result that

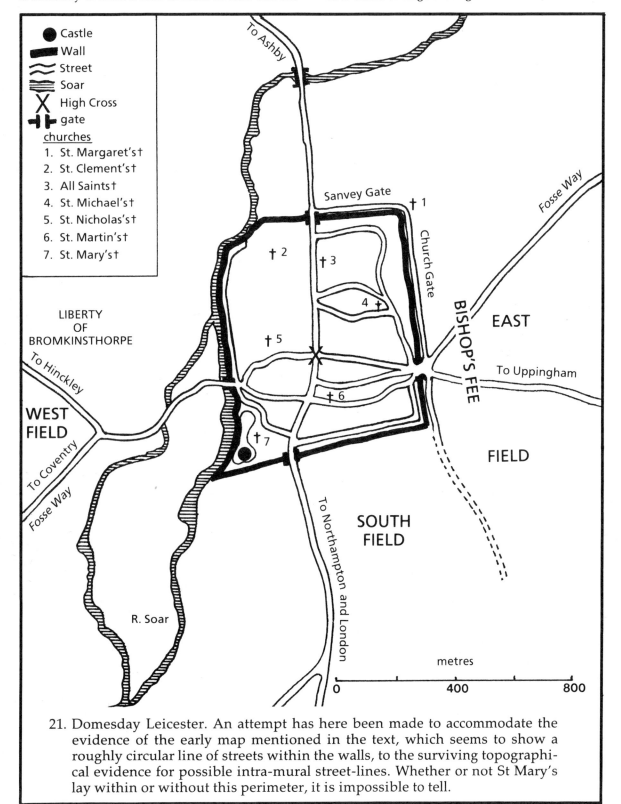

21. Domesday Leicester. An attempt has here been made to accommodate the evidence of the early map mentioned in the text, which seems to show a roughly circular line of streets within the walls, to the surviving topographical evidence for possible intra-mural street-lines. Whether or not St Mary's lay within or without this perimeter, it is impossible to tell.

Leicester, as one of these, received special treatment. Elsewhere in the shire settlements are described under the Tenants-in-Chief, wapentake by wapentake, but Leicester is taken out to form a completely separate section attached to no wapentake. This provides problems of interpretation which cannot be resolved by comparison with other Leicestershire entries, problems which cannot always be definitively settled. Even the titling is different. Leicester is described as *Civitas*, usually translated as "City" though Leicester at the time was not, as it once had been, an ecclesiastical see. Certainly *civitas* implies something very different from what *burgus* – a town – would. The entry then describes the payments, or renders, to the crown at the time of King Eadward (the Confessor) and now under King William, but insofar as these bear some similarity to the manorial valuations recorded in the countryside, they are mentioned at the beginning rather than, as with the rest of the shire, at the end of the entry. These renders and their significance are dealt with elsewhere (p.11), but it is noteworthy that they include services as well as rents in cash and kind under Eadward which have become entirely fiscal under William, so some tidying up seems already to have taken place by 1086. They also include a substantial rent from the moneyers of the mint, the possession of which was one mark of early borough status (inset 4). A third of this rent was already payable to Hugh of Grandmesnil, the leading figure in both the shire and the town, and thus the precursor of those who later, in the twelfth century, became the Earls of Leicester.

inset 4 Money: coins and the Domesday record . . . . R. A. Rutland

The basic commodity to survive from this period is money and it nicely combines archaeology and history since each coin is a small historical document in its own right. In one respect the coinage of this period is simple. It consisted solely of silver pennies which could be physically cut into two to produce halfpennies or into four to produce farthings (fourths). This may appear to be a strange practice but it makes more sense when one realises that each coin was worth its weight in silver. Far stranger is the realisation that when payment had to be made in cash, no matter how large the amount, the payment had to be made in pennies. Thus in 991 when the *Danegeld*, the money paid by the English to buy off Danish raids, was set at £10,000 this would have involved the physical handing over of 2,400,000 pennies, and in subsequent years the amount increased. It is not surprising, therefore, that in other financial transactions "money of account" was used, that is higher denominations for which there was no actual coin. This money of account varied from region to region so that it was always necessary to specify what you meant. Thus near the beginning of the Leicester Domesday entry we find this item

"From the moneyers (King William has) twenty pounds yearly of twenty to the *ora*"

This tells us that the writer is using the Danish *ora* of twenty pence as his money of account.

One of the questions asked by those compiling the Domesday entries was "How much is it worth?" This echoes the obvious question that one asks about money at any period in the past. The answer, however, is by no means simple. In the first place, when money is mentioned in contemporary documents it is often difficult to think of a modern equivalent with which to make a comparison. The entry quoted above, for example, indicates that the king receives £20 (4,800 pence) annually from the Leicester mint. Rather like modern rateable value this sort of information only allows us to make relative comparisons. It does not actually tell us what money was worth. The second difficulty is that it was not a wage economy so we cannot say how much people earned. Related to this is the fact that in many respects people were self-sufficient and not therefore as dependent as we are upon buying products for their daily needs. Finally the relative values of items within society were often quite different from what they are today. A good example of this is the buying power of the *mancus*, an amount of gold equivalent of 30 silver pence. We learn that in the late Saxon period it could buy three acres of land in the East Midlands. However we also hear of someone spending 120 *mancuses* of gold on a necklace. In other words, the necklace was worth 360 acres of land. Elsewhere we find that for the same amount one could purchase 120 oxen, 600 sheep or even 15 male slaves. None of this really helps us to understand the value of money at Domesday in terms which relate to our lives. It does however give some idea of both the use and value of money in the economy.

If we turn to the money itself we find that it has something important to say about the Norman Conquest. The penny had been the unit of currency since the eighth century, and the currency system in use at the Norman Conquest can be traced back to the reforms of Eadgar in 973. In fact the principles laid down by Eadgar survived basically intact through to the period of Henry II (1154–1189), and were therefore unaffected by the Conquest. Continuity from the Saxon into the Norman period therefore occurred not simply at the level of everyday life but in institutions directly under royal control.

Each coin was struck by hand between a pair of metal dies. The obverse showed the king's head with his name and title in Latin (King of the English). The reverse often had a design including a cross and the name of the mint and moneyer. The control of dies and coin types was centrally maintained, although there were up to 60 mints around the country, including Leicester, producing coins. At regular intervals, six years at first but later as little as two, a universal recoinage was carried out with new dies. Coins of previous issues were "demonetised" and had to be surrendered for restriking. This system was so well established that in 1069, despite the trauma of the Norman Conquest and the replacement of English lords by Normans, the recoinage due in that year took place as normal under moneyers who had operated under Eadward the Confessor. In Leicester, for example, we find Aegelwine and Godric minting coins under both Eadward and William.

(a) (b) (c)

(d) (e) (f)

22. Silver Pennies of Eadward the Confessor (1042–1066) and William the Conqueror (1066–1087) – enlarged.

(a) Eadweard wearing a radiate crown. Moneyer, Wulfric of Leicester.
(b) Eadweard (reverse). PACX (Peace) in angles of a cross. Moneyer, Wulfnoth of Leicester.
(c) Eadweard wearing a pointed helmet. Moneyer, Aegelric of Leicester.
(d) Eadweard (reverse). Pyramids in angles of a cross. Moneyer, Aelfsig of Chester.
(e) William (reverse). PAXS (Peace) in angles of a cross. Moneyer, Aelfsi of Chester – who may have been the same person as Aelfsig in (d).
(f) William crowned and holding a sceptre. Moneyer, Sunoulf of Chester.

The complex entry for Leicester which deserves now to be summarized according to its own sequence, then proceeds to describe not ploughlands but houses: the only houses referred to in the Leicestershire Domesday. Here the entry adopts – ideally, but not in practice – the standard form of dealing with the holdings of the tenants-in-chief in their feudal order. In this respect the Leicester entry may be similar to many other shire towns, but in one major respect it differs. If most other towns could describe themselves as royal boroughs, at Leicester the majority of the houses were already in other than royal hands. "Many county towns", says Mary Bateson, referring to a period only slightly later "knew what it was to have their castle in the hands of an Earl, but not many had in their midst an Earl who was also Lord of the borough." In Leicester, the King had only 39 houses in his own right, the Archbishop of York had but 2, Earl Hugh of Chester (but not of

Leicester) 17, the Abbot of Coventry 10, the Abbot of Crowland 3. Already therefore the monastic orders had property within the town. Most significantly, however, there then follows the holding of Hugh of Grandmesnil who, although not the Earl of Leicester was the castellan of its castle and the sheriff of its shire, had no fewer than 110 houses and two churches. Besides these he held 24 houses in common with the king, and it is not even clear whether these last formed part of the king's meagre total of 39 dwellings or not. Further, Hugh also had a number of houses which were attached to settlements outside in the shire, some 61 in all, and 37 burgesses in the town who were attached in some way to Anstey and Sileby. But were these 37 accommodated in some form of housing not attached to the outside settlements? The relation of burgesses to houses is not clear and it may be that although in other cases in the town, Hugh owned the houses he may not have had full control of their occupants. (It should be added that such problems of interpretation may simply be a matter of imperfect recording.) Hugh also had a further two churches, two more houses (were these for the priests serving the churches?) and four decayed ones. The need to enter decayed houses is obscure – perhaps, as in other towns, they had been destroyed to make room for the castle – but they may simply have been included to preserve Hugh's right to them. He had already a subtenant for five more houses. Then come nine houses belonging to Robert of Vessey and one of Geoffrey of La Guerche. Next are six which, attached to outside settlements, seem to have had no overlord within the town – and were presumably the properties – of the overlords of the settlements concerned. This part of the Leicester sequence ends with the mysterious statement that two lords who had lands in the shire, but no known houses in the town, had between them one burgess.

The last two entries for Leicester, when taken in conjunction with that for the related holding of the Bishop of Lincoln (which occurs elsewhere amongst the entries for the county), furnish significant additional information. The last Leicester holding to be mentioned belonged to the Countess Judith who is credited with 28 houses and the rent of half a mill "in the borough", together with six carucates of land "outside", and "pertaining" to it. The presence of ploughs, meadow and woodland on this estate, shows that, despite its urban status, the town thus had a supporting agricultural area, a point which is reinforced by the evidence for the Bishop of Lincoln's holding. This comprised 10 carucates on which nine ploughs were at work, a mill and half a mill (was this the other half of the Countess's?) plus two churches and 17 burgesses. For one piece of land "outside the wall", moreover, he had rent, a priest, three villeins and 12 bordars. He thus had not only property within the town but a substantial holding outside it as well. The Leicester entry itself ends with a reference to the woodland called *Hereswode*, in which (if, as is usually assumed, it was Leicester Forest) much later evidence suggests that the citizens may have had fuel-gathering and other customary rights.

At Domesday therefore Leicester was already the pre-eminent settlement in the county and it was a walled town. The archaeological evidence suggests that the Roman walls of the early town determine the layout of the later medieval walls. This is deducible from a fifteenth-century survey and there is no reason to surmise that the early medieval walls were on any different alignment. In this case the walled area would have enclosed about 130 acres. Within the walls were at least 322 houses, and probably nearer 400 if the various burgesses referred to all had houses which are not included in the first total. The occupants of these houses owned allegiance to several different overlords, the King, Earl Hugh of Chester, the Countess Judith and others, but the most substantial was Hugh of Grandmesnil.

Is the Domesday entry for Leicester comprehensive? As will appear later it does not include some vital things which must then have existed. In the rest of the shire, recording goes down to the humblest levels and the Bishop of Lincoln's entry includes bordars on land attached to the town. Were these the only bordars in the town's area? Elsewhere, many cottagers are recorded as at least adjacent to towns, whereas at Leicester only burgesses are designated. Were these last the same as the occupiers of houses? What other social levels were there? It is conceivable that the lowest stratum of the inhabitants, who were considered totally unprofitable, may not have been recorded at all.

Such considerations apart, the number of houses detailed, if it does represent a fairly complete account, suggests a total population of about 2,000 or of that order, one which would by no means fill the city's present de Montfort Hall. How and where were these 322 or 380 houses, 6 churches and two mills distributed about the town? It is certain that two main streets existed, one running north/south from the Northgate, beyond All Saints church, to the Southgate; one running east/west from the west gate (roughly the west bridge) to the Eastgate. These intersected at the High Cross, somewhat off the geometrical centre but for centuries the main focus of the town. Behind and around them ran a number of lanes some of which developed into the street pattern which lasted from the twelfth to the twentieth centuries. There is some slight indication from a somewhat later map that the early built-up area had a roughly circular defining perimeter bank or trackway within the confines of the walls but there has so far been no archaeological confirmation of this. The limited extent of the population makes this not impossible.

Six churches are mentioned as existing in Domesday within the town while the Bishop of Lincoln's holding outside included a priest. This latter and the evidence of a church previous to the present one on the site of St Margaret's suggests that the suburb had its own religious and ecclesiastical provision: in later times, indeed, an area broadly equivalent to that of this parish became known as the Bishop's Fee. The identities of the other six churches are not certain, but All Saints, St Martin's, St Mary's and St Nicholas would have been included, plus probably two in the northern part of the town, St Clement's and St Michael's, which did not survive much beyond the end of the Middle Ages. Just how far the parishes were defined at Domesday is not clear as the parish system was not fully developed until the twelfth century. At a time when any person of wealth or influence could establish a church perhaps these represent six major holdings from the pre-conquest period and the later parishes coalesced around them. The boundary between St Nicholas and St Martin's ran for one stretch along the line of a robbed out Roman wall which would have formed an early and obvious division.

Dr Martin has argued from the distribution of the churches in the medieval period that the early concentration of houses was densest in the area north of the High Cross towards All Saints. Further, it has often been asserted that the north-east quarter of the town had once been populous but suffered most in the sack of the town during the rebellion of 1173 and that thereafter it was desolate until the nineteenth century. So far, however, there has been no archaeological evidence that the north-east quarter was densely populated before the sack. What is certain is that the intra-mural houses would have occupied only a tiny fraction of the ground area of the town and that large portions must have been waste or open.

There is also the disputed question of the Bishop of Lincoln's Leicester holding. This property, insofar as it may be associated with St Margaret's parish, was presumably to be considered as part of the town though outside the walls. On the one hand it has been suggested that the Bishop's holding reflected a policy, during the reconquest of the Danelaw, of handing over large Danish tracts to a great landowner or to the church, and that consequently the Bishop's holding basically represents the Danish area as it was originally settled *outside* the walls. This is quite possible especially as this eastern suburb would have had good communications with the Wreake valley where place-names suggest very heavy Danish occupation. It is equally possible, on the other hand, that Hugh of Grandmesnil's intra-mural holding also had a similar origin and thus represents the transference to a Mercian lord of the main area *within* the walls (p.19). An explanation of this kind might better account for the size of such a non-royal holding in the town which otherwise must remain a puzzling anomaly. If that was the case, the dichotomy between a presumed Danish area outside the walls and an Anglo-Saxon one within them would disappear and a mixture of Danes and English could reasonably be postulated in both. Certainly a *mélange* of languages would have obtained at the time of Domesday – Old English, Danish, Norman-French, while literate people communicating in these three languages would have been able to record any decisions in a fourth, Latin.

Around the town, as implied in the Bishop's and the Countess Judith's holdings, there existed an agricultural supporting area which, either by then or later, developed into the three town-fields that are evidenced from a slightly later date. Nevertheless, the thrust of urban life which differentiated it from that of a rural vill, was the town's commercial activity combined with its function as an administrative and judicial centre.

The first of these two roles does not appear to have been of much interest to the royal commissioners. No market is mentioned in Domesday nor is any indication of the profits to be produced by the town's commercial activity, but a document only twenty years after Domesday shows something of the antiquity and organisation of this. By a charter of 1107 Robert of Beaumont, Count of Meulan, who had acquired the lordship, granted to his merchants of Leicester that they should hold their Gild with all the customs as they had held it in the time of King William and his son William and now under King Henry. The "Merchant Gild" therefore goes back at least to William I's time or before, and this argues an organised commercial community back to or before our period. This commercial organisation inevitably implies a market. The Gild was an attempt to control and regulate trading, excluding non-members from privileges and extracting concessions from would-be members. It may well be that the attachment of urban houses to outside settlements, in and by the time of Domesday, indicates the value of trading privileges in those cases where trading rights were attached to specific houses that gave access to the market from the settlements concerned. The earliest market was at the High Cross, the centre of the town, and only later was the present market area brought into use as markets eventually migrated eastwards to it. Indeed, when compared with the older built-up area around the High Cross, the layout of the property boundaries around the present market place, which lasted right down into this century, has suggested that that area only became densely inhabited as late as the twelfth century.

The second major role to be performed by a shire town had to do with justice and administration. It is not known whether the shire court actually met at this time in Leicester, but it is certain that the "city" itself was controlled from the castle which had been built *c.* 1068 and whose construction had greatly affected the south-west corner of the town. The castle was only twenty years old at Domesday, the mound still fresh and the presumed wooden defensive palisade still on top overlooking and threatening as well as perhaps offering defence to this militarily strategic town. Probably its construction had involved the destruction of a former collegiate church in the area, while its very existence now imported a new and continuing link with the feudal overlordship. Apparently constructed by the crown originally, by 1086 it was already the centre of the Grandmesnil power in the area.

From the grants which the townsmen obtained from the later lords of the castle it is clear that at an early date some predecessor of the latter had been owed services like an ordinary manorial lord. The townsmen had been required to reap his corn, to compensate him for damage done by their cattle, to have their corn ground at his mill, to have bread baked at this bakehouse, to pay rents to him for their tenements. They had early obtained exemption from the new Norman procedure of trial by battle and could have cases determined by a jury of 24, perhaps a carryover of "lawmen" from the Danish period (p.7). Houses fronting the then High Street had paid a special rent which may indicate the original nucleus of the built-up area.

Whatever services and rents, as predecessor of the later Earls, Hugh of Grandmesnil may have extracted in the eleventh century, it is clear that any tendency for Leicester to be reduced to the status of a manor was later resisted by the townsmen whose financial power enabled them slowly to assert their burghal independence. Indeed a charter of the mid-twelfth century acknowledged the rights of the Portmanmoot as the pre-eminent court of the town, and this was the court of the townsmen, not of the feudal overlord. It heard not only cases between townsmen but was to develop into a land court and became formally a Court of Record on December 26 1199. It is in the functioning of the Portmanmoot that we can dimly discern the forerunner of the later governing body. The distinction between the Portmanmoot and the Gild Merchant may have been that between the judicial and commercial functions of the town, but in practice the membership of the ruling bodies of each may simply have involved a changing of hats by the same "maior et sanior" townsmen. Certainly the moves towards the control of their own affairs which in many towns took the form of acquiring the "Firma Burgi" (financial independence from the Crown), was in Leicester a series of gradual moves by the townsmen in extracting privileges from the Earl.

The picture that emerges from Domesday and documents of an early date, is of a town of about 2,000 souls all told, mainly contained within its walls but with a flourishing suburb on the east side, all set within an agricultural area. It did not live entirely by trade but it was mainly its commercial position which distinguished it from the rest of the shire. This commercial life was active and well-organised and the town was soon trying to free itself from total feudal dependence on its overlord who, unlike many towns of a similar size in the country, was not the king. The inhabitants were a mixture of Anglo-Saxons and Danes with the latter not necessarily being restricted to the suburb. The physical layout of the town was already fairly well defined with a street pattern which would last for nearly 800 years. Its religious needs were met by six or possibly seven churches, one for every 280 inhabitants. It had two mills and an established if rudimentary administrative system. Finally, Leicester was the shire town and as such was, and would remain, the dominant urban grouping in that shire.

CONCLUSION

Editor

The first stage of the Norman Conquest involved a process of usually brutal superimpositions by an alien order on an existing society. It brought with it the displacement of the Old English greater nobility, and the replacement in the provinces of English bishops, English abbots, and English sheriffs by Normans: the English moneyers alone appear to have survived as a recognisable group at this public level. Above all, the Conquest involved the most sudden and the most profound change in landownership to be documented in English history. For the victors in general it brought wealth and power that was probably unrivalled in Europe. In England their extensive new estates left little room for the smaller thegnly landholder who had characterised a minor but noticeable element in the landed patterns of pre-Conquest society. From the new estates, rewards for followers had to be found – as time went on, even for tenants from across the channel – with all that that meant for the multiplication of sub-tenancies. If that process in its turn may have helped to accelerate an existing trend towards manorialisation, one outcome of this and of other factors was the eventual depression of the indigenous "free" peasantry.

Yet these were basically all features of, or set in train by, the first stage of Conquest. Once the take-over had been accomplished, it was William's deliberate policy to perpetuate the structures of the society he had conquered. And it is a fact that should be remarked, that the English population as a whole broadly adapted itself within less than a generation to the transition. In 1088, two years after Domesday Book, English forces actually fought for William's successor, Rufus, against the rebellious Odo of Bayeux. Most remarkable of all, given the absence of a large scale migration from Normandy, is the revolution in personal naming that was already becoming apparent by 1100 in London and amongst landholders elsewhere. The christian names of Anglo-Saxon England, which now seem like tongue-twisters, were by then already being replaced with names such as William, Richard and John. Inter-marriage between Norman and English was clearly widespread by the early twelfth century.

For what began as a superimposition, continued slowly but increasingly as a fusion of two cultures. It was not after all in the interests of the new Norman landholding class to beggar the estates from which their incomes were drawn. Between 1066 and 1086 in those counties where Domesday provides the information, the numbers of slaves were not in fact hugely swollen; they decreased markedly. It might be argued, moreover, that in many cases Norman vitality helped to energise and so accelerate pre-existing trends: trends towards new town foundations; towards the increase in rural marketing and trade; and, at least where deliberate planning was involved, towards the formation of villages and common-fields.

In lasting material terms, the legacy of this extraordinary breed of adventurers still lies all around us for those that have eyes to see. It is there in the soil; in the tumescent mounds of their barbaric castles as at Leicester or near Uppingham; in the banks they flung up to protect their hunting-rights (some of which in the region may date further back than is sometimes supposed); and, it may well prove, in the lay-outs of some of our villages and fields. The legacy is still there both on the map and on the tongue in Leicestershire (but significantly not in Rutland), where places like Kibworth Beauchamp and Kibworth Harcourt, Stonton Wyville and Dunton Bassett all recall the names of first or second generation Normans. Even Belgrave was re-named because the Normans thought one element of its Old English name, "Merdegrave" (which actually means "the grove inhabited by martins"), sounded too much like the French word for "shit". The legacy is there in the buildings they left behind and which reflect that fusion of design which is neither English nor purely Norman: in parts of St Mary de Castro in Leicester and, rather later, in a number of churches in Rutland like those at Egleton or Tickencote; and in two remarkable domestic buildings that are ultimately expressive of these developments: the uniquely surviving hall of Oakham castle within its embanked fortification; and parts of the Great Hall of Leicester Castle. The legacy is there even more personally in the chapel of Belvoir Castle, where now lies the empty and echoing sarcophagus of no less a figure than Robert of Tosny – in 1086, the holder of 16 manors in Leicestershire and one in Rutland; the builder of the earliest castle at Belvoir; the founder of Belvoir priory (a cell of St Albans) and, some would claim, the standard-bearer of William the Conqueror himself. But the greatest legacy of all from that age is more than material: it lies as a silent challenge to the curious in the folios of that massive tome which now we know as Domesday Book.

A Guide to Further Reading

Abbreviation   V.C.H.: Victoria County History

General Background

(in order of appearance):

F. M. Stenton, *Anglo-Saxon England*, Oxford, 3rd edn., 1971.
P. H. Sawyer, *From Roman Britain to Norman England*, London, 1978.
David Hill, *An Atlas of Anglo-Saxon England*, Oxford, 1984.
Marjorie Chibnall, *Anglo-Norman England 1066–1166*, Oxford, 1986.

Domesday Book (1) *Introductions:*
R. Welldon Finn, *An Introduction to Domesday Book*, London, 1963.
R. Welldon Finn, *Domesday Book: A Guide*, London and Chichester, 1973.

Domesday Book (2) *Accessible translations of regional texts:*
The most accurate, with pioneering introductions which now require some modification, are:
F. M. Stenton, "Domesday Survey" in *V.C.H. Leicestershire*, I, London, 1907, pp. 277–338.
F. M. Stenton, "Domesday Survey" in *V.C.H. Rutland*, I, London, 1908, pp. 121–142.
Useful for their reprint of the latin text and some modern identifications are:
Philip Morgan, ed., *Domesday Book: Leicestershire*, Chichester, 1979 (being vol. 22 in John Morris, ed., *Domesday Book*).
Frank Thorn, ed., *Domesday Book: Rutland*, Chichester, 1980 (being vol. 29 in the same series).

The Leicestershire Survey
C. F. Slade, *The Leicestershire Survey c.A.D.1130: A New Edition*, University of Leicester, Department of English Local History Occasional Papers, first series, 7, 1956.

Suggested reading

(in the order of the chapters of this book) *in addition to* titles already cited.

PART I   DOMESDAY BOOK AND THE NORMAN CONQUEST

H. R. Loyn, *The Governance of Anglo-Saxon England 500–1087*, London, 1984.
V. H. Galbraith, *The Making of Domesday Book*, Oxford, 1961.
D. C. Douglas, *William the Conqueror*, London, 1964.
R. H. C. Davis, *The Normans and Their Myth*, London, 1976.

PART II   REGIONAL BACKGROUNDS TO DOMESDAY BOOK

1. Leicestershire and Rutland

F. M. Stenton, "The Danes in England" in D. M. Stenton, ed., *Preparatory to Anglo-Saxon England*, Oxford, 1970, pp. 136–165.
Pauline Stafford, *The East Midlands in the Early Middle Ages*, Studies in the Early History of Britain, Leicester, 1985.
Charles Phythian-Adams, "Rutland Reconsided" in Ann Dornier, ed., *Mercian Studies*, Leicester, 1977, pp. 63–84.
Charles Phythian-Adams, "The Emergence of Rutland and the Making of the Realm", *Rutland Record*, I, 1980, pp. 5–12.

2. Structures of Landholding

G. R. J. Jones, "Multiple Estates and Early Settlement" in P. H. Sawyer, ed., *English Medieval Settlement*, London, 1979, p.b., pp. 9–40.
W. G. Hoskins, *Leicestershire: An Illustrated Essay on the History of the Landscape*, London, 1957, pp. 6–11.
Charles Phythian-Adams, *Continuity, Fields and Fission: The Making of a Midland Parish*, University of Leicester, Department of English Local History Occasional Papers, 2nd ser., 4, 1978.
F. M. Stenton, *Types of Manorial Structure in the Northern Danelaw*, Oxford Studies in Social and legal History, Oxford, 1910.
G. W. S. Barrow, *The Kingdom of the Scots*, London, 1973, chapt. 1.

3. Lords and the Land

Peter Sawyer, "1066–1086: A Tenurial Revolution?" in Peter Sawyer, ed., *Domesday Book: A Reassessment*, London, 1985, pp. 71–85.

F. E. Harmer, "Judicial and Financial Rights" in F. E. Harmer, *Anglo-Saxon Writs*, Manchester, 1952, pp. 73–78.

Horace Round, *Feudal England*, London, 1895.

John Le Patourel, *The Norman Empire*, Oxford, 1976.

4. The Sorts and Conditions of People
F. W. Maitland, *Domesday Book and Beyond*, Cambridge, 1907.

Reginald Lennard, *Rural England 1086–1135*, Oxford, 1959.

H. P. R. Finberg, "Anglo-Saxon England to 1042" in H. P. R. Finberg, ed., *The Agrarian History of England and Wales, I, ii, A.D.43–1042*, Cambridge, 1972, pp. 507–525.

S. P. J. Harvey, "Evidence for Settlement Study: Domesday Book" in P. H. Sawyer, ed., *English Medieval Settlement*, London, 1979, p.b., pp. 105–109.

PART III: LEICESTERSHIRE AND RUTLAND IN THE LATE ELEVENTH CENTURY
1. Introduction
H. C. Darby, *Domesday England*, Cambridge, 1977.

R. Welldon Finn, *The Norman Conquest and its Effects on the Economy 1066–1086*, London, 1971.

Sally P. J. Harvey, "Taxation and the Ploughland in Domesday Book" in Peter Sawyer, ed., *Domesday Book: A Reassessment*, London, 1985, pp. 86–103.

Cyril Hart, *The Hidation of Northamptonshire*, University of Leicester, Department of English Local History Occasional Papers, 2nd ser., 3, 1970.

2. Population, Settlement and Rural Economy
General Background
Christopher Taylor, *Village and Farmstead: A History of Rural settlement in England*, London, 1983.

H. S. A. Fox, "Approaches to the Midland System", in Trevor Rowley, ed., *the Origins of Open-Field Agriculture*, London, 1981.

Alan Everitt, "The Wolds Once More", *Journal of Historical Geography*, 5, 1, 1979.

Oliver Rackham, *Trees and Woodland in the British Landscape*, London, 1976.

Alan Everitt, "The Primary Towns of England" in Alan Everitt, *Landscape and Community in England*, London, 1985, pp. 67–71.

Regional
D. Holly, "Leicestershire",

I. B. Terrett, "Rutland",

both in H. C. Darby, ed., *The Domesday Geography of Midland England*, Cambridge, 1971.

C. T. Smith, "Population", *V.C.H. Leicestershire*, III, London, 1955, pp. 128–217.

R. H. Hilton, "Medieval Agrarian History", *V.C.H. Leicestershire*, II, London, 1954, pp. 145–198.

Peter Liddle, *Leicestershire Archaeology – The Present State of Knowledge, 2, Anglo-Saxon and Medieval Periods*, Archaeological Reports ser., 5, Leicestershire Museums, 1982.

3. Churches and Churchgoing in 1086
F. Barlow, *The English Church 1000–1066*, London, 2nd edn., 1979.

C. J. Godfrey, *The Church in Anglo-Saxon England*, Cambridge, 1962.

E. C. Fernie, *The Architecture of the Anglo-Saxons*, London, 1983.

W. Page, "Some Remarks on the Churches of the Domesday Survey", *Archaeologia*, LXVI, 1915, pp. 61–102.

4. Leicester in Domesday
Jack Simmons, *Leicester Past and Present, I, Ancient Borough*, London, 1974.

Mary Bateson, ed., *Records of the Borough of Leicester, 1103–1327*, London, 1899, "Introduction".

G. H. Martin, "Church Life in Medieval Leicester" in A. E. Brown, ed., *The Growth of Leicester*, Leicester, 1970, chapt. 3.

G. H. Martin, "The Evolution of Leicester: Norman to Tudor" in N. Pye, ed., *Leicester and its Region*, Leicester, 1972.

Inset 4: Money
Michael Dolley, *Anglo-Saxon Pennies*, British Museum, 1970.

T. H. McK. Clough, Ann Dornier and R. A. Rutland, *Anglo-Saxon and Viking Leicestershire (including Rutland)*, Leicestershire Museums, 1975.

INDEX
OF REFERENCES TO TECHNICAL TERMS

NOTES